GENESIS to REVELATION

A Comprehensive Verse-by-Verse Exploration of the Bible

PSALMS

JOHN C. HOLBERT

LEADER GUIDE

GENESIS to REVELATION

A Comprehensive Verse-by-Verse Exploration of the Bible

PSALMS

JOHN C. HOLBERT

LEADER GUIDE

GENESIS TO REVELATION SERIES: **PSALMS**
LEADER GUIDE

ABINGDON PRESS

Nashville

Copyright © 1984, 1985, 1987 by Graded Press.

Revised Edition Copyright © 1997 by Abingdon Press.

Updated and Revised Edition Copyright © 2017 by Abingdon Press

All rights reserved.

ISBN 978-1-5018-4839-1

Manufactured in the United States of America

17 18 19 20 21 22 23 24 25 26—10 9 8 7 6 5 4 3 2 1

HOW TO TEACH GENESIS TO REVELATION

Unique Features of This Bible Study

In Genesis to Revelation, you and your class will study the Bible in three steps. Each step provides a different level of understanding of the Scripture. We call these steps Dimension One, Dimension Two, and Dimension Three.

Dimension One concerns what the Bible actually says. You do not interpret the Scripture at this point; you merely take account of what it says. Your main goal for this dimension is to get the content of the passage clear in your mind. What does the Bible say?

Dimension One is in workbook form. The members of the class will write the answers to questions about the passage in the space provided in the participant book. All the questions in Dimension One can be answered by reading the Bible itself. Be sure the class finishes Dimension One before going on to Dimensions Two and Three.

Dimension Two concerns information that will shed light on the Scripture under consideration. Dimension Two will answer such questions as

- What are the original meanings of some of the words used in the passage?
- What is the original background of the passage?
- Why was the passage most likely written?
- What are the relationships between the persons mentioned in the passage?
- What geographical and cultural factors affect the meaning of the passage?

The question for Dimension Two is, What information do we need in order to understand the meaning of the passage? In Dimension One the class members will discover what the Bible says. In Dimension Two they will discover what the Bible means.

Dimension Three focuses on interpreting the Scripture and applying it to life situations. The questions here are

- What is the meaning of the passage for my life?
- What response does the passage require of me as a Christian?
- What response does this passage require of us as a group?

Dimension Three questions have no easy answers. The task of applying the Scripture to life situations is up to you and the class.

Aside from the three-dimensional approach, another unique feature of this study is the organization of the series as a whole. Classes that choose to study the Genesis to Revelation Series will be able to study all the books of the Bible in their biblical order. This method will give the class continuity that is not present in most other Bible studies. The class will read and study virtually every verse of the Bible, from Genesis straight through to Revelation.

Weekly Preparation

Begin planning for each session early in the week. Read the passage that the lesson covers, and write the answers to Dimension One questions in the participant book. Then read Dimensions Two and Three in the participant book. Make a note of any questions or comments you have. Finally, study the material in the leader guide carefully. Decide how you want to organize your class session.

Organizing the Class Session

Since Genesis to Revelation involves three steps in studying the Scripture, you will want to organize your class sessions around these three dimensions. Each lesson in the participant book and this leader guide consists of three parts.

The first part of each lesson in the leader guide is the same as the Dimension One section in the participant book, except that the leader guide includes the answers to Dimension One questions. These questions and answers are taken from the New International Version of the Bible.

You might use Dimension One in several ways:

1. Ask the group members to read the Scripture and to write the answers to all the Dimension One questions before coming to class. This method will require that the class covenant to spend the necessary amount of study time outside of class. When the class session begins, read through the Dimension One questions, asking for responses from the group members. If anyone needs help with any of the answers, look at the biblical reference together.

2. Or, if you have enough class time, you might spend the first part of the session working through the Dimension One questions together as a group. Locate the Scripture references, ask the questions one at a time, and invite the class members to find the answers and to read them aloud. Then allow enough time for them to write the answers in the participant book.

3. Or, take some time at the beginning of the class session for group members to work individually. Have them read the Dimension One questions and the Scripture references and then write their answers to the questions in the spaces provided in the participant book. Discuss together any questions or answers in Dimension One that do not seem clear. This approach may take longer than the others, but it provides a good change of pace from time to time.

You do not have to organize your class sessions the same way every week. Ask the class members what they prefer. Experiment! You may find ways to study the Dimension One material other than the ones listed above.

The second part of each lesson in this leader guide corresponds to the second part of the participant book lessons. The Dimension Two section of the participant book provides background information to help the participants understand the Scripture. Become familiar with the information in the participant book.

Dimension Two of this leader guide contains additional information on the passage. The leader guide goes into more depth with some parts of the passage than the participant book does. You will want to share this information with the group in whatever way seems appropriate. For example, if someone raises a question about a particular verse, share any additional background information from the leader guide.

You might raise a simple question such as, What words or phrases gave you trouble in understanding the passage? or, Having grasped the content of the passage, what questions remain in your mind? Encourage the group members to share confusing points, troublesome words or phrases, or lingering questions. Write these problems on a posterboard or markerboard. This list of concerns will form the outline for the second portion of the session.

These concerns may also stimulate some research on the part of the group members. If your study group is large enough, divide the class into three groups. Then divide the passage for the following week into three parts. Assign a portion of the passage to each group. Using Bible commentaries and Bible dictionaries, direct each group to discover as much as it can about this portion of the passage before the class meets again. Each group will then report its findings during the class session.

The third part of each lesson in this leader guide relates to Dimension Three in the participant book. This section helps class members discover how to apply the Scripture to their own lives. Here you will find one or more interpretations of the passage—whether traditional, historical, or contemporary. Use these interpretations when appropriate to illumine the passage for the group members.

Dimension Three in the participant book points out some of the issues in the passage that are relevant to our lives. For each of these issues, the participant book raises questions to help the participants assess the meaning of the Scripture for their lives. The information in Dimension Three of the leader guide is designed to help you lead the class in discussing these issues. Usually, you will find a more in-depth discussion of portions of the Scripture.

The discussion in the leader guide will give you a better perspective on the Scripture and its interpretation before you begin to assess its meaning for today. You will probably want to share this Dimension Three information with the class to open the discussion. For each life situation, the leader guide contains suggestions on facilitating the class discussion. You, as the leader, are responsible for group discussions of Dimension Three issues.

Assembling Your Materials

You will need at least three items to prepare for and conduct each class session:

- A leader guide

- A participant book

- A Bible—you may use any translation or several; the answers in this leader guide are taken from the New International Version.

One advantage of the Genesis to Revelation Series is that the study is self-contained. That is, all you need to teach this Bible study is provided for you in the participant books and leader guides. Occasionally, or perhaps on a regular basis, you might want to consult other sources for additional information.

HOW TO LEAD A DISCUSSION

The Teacher as Discussion Leader

As the leader of this series or a part of this series, one of your main responsibilities during each class period will be to lead the class discussion. Some leaders are apprehensive about leading a discussion. In many ways, it is easier to lecture to the class. But remember that the class members will surely benefit more from the class sessions when they actively participate in a discussion of the material.

Leading a discussion is a skill that any leader can master with practice. And keep in mind—especially if your class is not used to discussion—that the members of your group will also be learning through practice. The following are some pointers on how to lead interesting and thought-provoking discussions in the study group.

Preparing for a Discussion—Where Do I Start?

1. Focus on the subject that will be discussed and on the goal you want to achieve through that discussion.

2. Prepare by collecting information and data that you will need; jot down these ideas, facts, and questions so that you will have them when you need them.

3. Begin organizing your ideas; stop often to review your work. Keep in mind the climate within the group—attitudes, feelings, eagerness to participate and learn.

4. Consider possible alternative group procedures. Be prepared for the unexpected.

5. Having reached your goal, think through several ways to bring the discussion to a close.

6. As the leader, do not feel that your responsibility is to give a full account or report of the assigned material. This practice promotes dependency. Instead, through stimulating questions and discussion, the participants will read the material—not because you tell them to but because they want to read and prepare.

How Do I Establish a Climate for Learning?

The leader's readiness and preparation quickly establish a climate in which the group can proceed and its members learn and grow. The anxiety and fear of an unprepared leader are contagious but so are the positive vibrations coming from a leader who is prepared to move into a learning enterprise.

An attitude of shared ownership is also basic. Group members need to perceive themselves as part of the learning experience. Persons establish ownership by working on goals, sharing concerns, and accepting major responsibility for learning.

Here are several ways the leader can foster a positive climate for learning and growth.

1. Readiness. A leader who is always fully prepared can promote, in turn, the group's readiness to learn.

2. Exploration. When the leader encourages group members to freely explore new ideas, persons will know they are in a group whose primary function is learning.

3. Exposure. A leader who is open, honest, and willing to reveal himself or herself to the group will encourage participants to discuss their feelings and opinions.

4. Confidentiality. A leader can create a climate for learning when he or she respects the confidentiality of group members and encourages the group members to respect one another's confidentiality.

5. Acceptance. When a leader shows a high degree of acceptance, participants can likewise accept one another honestly.

How Can I Deal With Conflict?

What if conflict or strong disagreement arises in your group? What do you do? Think about the effective and ineffective ways you have dealt with conflict in the past.

Group conflict may come from one of several sources. One common source of conflict involves personality clashes. Any group is almost certain to contain at least two persons whose personalities clash. If you break your class into smaller groups for discussion, be sure these persons are in separate groups.

Another common source of group conflict is subject matter. The Bible can be a very controversial subject. Remember the difference between discussion or disagreement and conflict. As a leader you will have to decide when to encourage discussion and when to discourage conflict that is destructive to the group process.

Group conflict may also come from a general atmosphere conducive to expression of ideas and opinions. Try to discourage persons in the group from being judgmental toward others and their ideas. Keep reminding the class that each person is entitled to his or her own opinions and that no one opinion is more valid than another.

How Much Should I Contribute to the Discussion?

Many leaders are unsure about how much they should contribute to the class discussions. Below are several pitfalls to avoid.

1. The leader should remain neutral on a question until the group has had adequate time to discuss it. At the proper time in the discussion the leader can offer his or her opinion. The leader can direct the questions to the group at large, rechanneling those questions that come to him or her.

   At times when the members need to grapple with a question or issue, the most untimely response a leader can make is answering the question. Do not fall into the trap of doing the group members' work for them. Let them struggle with the question.

   However, if the leader has asked the group members to reveal thoughts and feelings, then group members have the right to expect the same of the leader. A leader has no right to ask others to reveal something he or she is unwilling to reveal. A leader can reveal thoughts and feelings, but at the appropriate time.

   The refusal to respond immediately to a question often takes self-discipline. The leader has spent time thinking, reading, and preparing. Thus the leader usually does have a point of view, and waiting for others to respond calls for restraint.

2. Another pitfall is the leader's making a speech or extended comments in expressing an opinion or summarizing what has been said. For example, in an attempt to persuade others, a leader may speak, repeat, or strongly emphasize what someone says concerning a question.

3. Finally, the pitfall of believing the leader must know "the answers" to the questions is always apparent. The leader need not know all the answers. Many questions that should be raised are ultimate and unanswerable; other questions are open-ended; and still others have several answers.

GENESIS TO REVELATION SERIES
PSALMS Leader Guide

Table of Contents

About the Writer

John C. Holbert wrote these lessons on Psalms. Dr. Holbert, an ordained United Methodist minister, served as Professor Emeritus of Homiletics at Perkins School of Theology, Southern Methodist University. His teaching specialties were in preaching, Hebrew Bible, and literature and preaching.

OUTLINE FOR THE PSALMS

Unlike most of the units in the Genesis to Revelation Series, this unit on the Psalms does not proceed straight through the Book of Psalms. Instead, you and the class members will study the psalms by categories. In this way, you will be able to study each psalm along with other psalms that are similar to it. This method will enable you to grasp both the similarity and the diversity among the psalms.

An outline showing which psalms will be covered in each lesson is provided for you here. In addition, you will want to read the section on pages 13–16 entitled "Introduction to the Psalms." These pages will give you general information that will be useful when introducing the Book of Psalms to the class members.

LESSON ONE: HYMNS OF PRAISE
Psalms 8, 19, 29, 33, 47, 93, 95, 96, 97, 98, 99, 104

LESSON TWO: HYMNS OF PRAISE
Psalms 113, 114, 115, 117, 121, 134, 135, 145, 146, 147, 148, 149, 150

LESSON THREE: SONGS OF ZION
Psalms 15, 24, 46, 48, 76, 84, 87, 122, 132

LESSON FOUR: ROYAL PSALMS
Psalms 2, 18, 20, 21, 45, 72, 89, 101, 110, 144

LESSON FIVE: COMMUNAL THANKSGIVING PSALMS
Psalms 65, 66, 67, 75, 100, 105, 106, 107, 124, 136

LESSON SIX: INDIVIDUAL THANKSGIVING PSALMS
Psalms 30, 32, 34, 40, 41, 92, 103, 111, 116, 118, 138

LESSON SEVEN: INDIVIDUAL LAMENTS
Psalms 3, 4, 5, 6, 7, 9, 10, 13, 14, 17, 22, 25

LESSON EIGHT: INDIVIDUAL LAMENTS
Psalms 26, 27, 28, 31, 35, 36, 38, 39, 42, 43, 51, 52, 53

LESSON NINE: INDIVIDUAL LAMENTS
Psalms 54, 55, 56, 57, 58, 59, 61, 63, 64, 69, 70, 71, 77

LESSON TEN: INDIVIDUAL LAMENTS
Psalms 86, 88, 94, 102, 108, 109, 120, 130, 139, 140, 141, 142, 143

LESSON ELEVEN: COMMUNAL LAMENTS
Psalms 12, 44, 60, 74, 79, 80, 83, 85, 90, 123, 125, 126, 129, 137

LESSON TWELVE: WISDOM PSALMS
Psalms 1, 37, 49, 73, 78, 91, 112, 119, 127, 128, 133

LESSON THIRTEEN: PSALMS OF CONFIDENCE
Psalms 11, 16, 23, 62, 131

MISCELLANEOUS PSALMS
Psalms 50, 68, 81, 82

INTRODUCTION TO THE PSALMS

In his book *How Came the Bible?* (Abingdon, 1940, 1976) Edgar Goodspeed says, "No book in the Bible is so dear to modern devotion as the Psalms." Perhaps the Psalms are so beloved because they reflect the human condition at its strongest. They speak of the fullest joy and praise. They speak of the depths of sorrow and fear. The psalmists speak of God and to God in praise, in thanksgiving, and in petition. As religious poetry, the Psalms are an integral part of the dialogue between humans and God.

Title

Our English title *Psalms* comes from the Latin *psalmi* (songs) that comes from the title in the Septuagint (an ancient Greek translation). In Hebrew, the Psalms are called praises or songs of praise.

Authorship and Setting

Jewish tradition assumes that David wrote the psalms because he is said to have composed songs and hymns to God. The New Testament follows this assumption. Some of the psalms are David's (for example Psalms 3–9, 11–32), but not all of them (see Psalm 72:20). The psalm titles name various authors, including David, the choirmaster, the Sons of Korah, and Asaph. These titles were probably added some time after the psalms themselves were written but before the Christian era. David's songs probably served as models for later writers. The Psalms were written under varying circumstances over many generations.

The Psalms often speak of singing, of musical instruments, and of temple activities. Many probably were written for use in worship services or were adapted for worship. Members of the temple staff or prophets who were associated with the temple may have written some of these community psalms. For example, Nehemiah 12:27 tells us that Levites came to the dedication of the walls of Jerusalem under Nehemiah to celebrate "with songs of thanksgiving and with the music of cymbals, harps and lyres."

Some psalms came from individual need. They are personal, devotional poetry that came to be part of Scripture. They originally may have been used by individuals for special ceremonies during worship services. An example of this special kind of psalm is found in the story of Hannah in 1 Samuel 1–2. Hannah prayed for a child, and after her son's birth she and her family went to the house of the Lord to worship. There Hannah offered a prayer, a psalm of praise to the greatness of the Lord (1 Samuel 2:1-10).

Collections in the Psalter

Individual psalms may have first been gathered into collections smaller than our present book since some psalms and parts of psalms are repeated. (For example, see Psalm 14 and Psalm 53.) Also, thirty-four psalms have no title and twenty-eight of these are found between Psalm 91 and Psalm 150. There are no musical terms in the titles of Psalms 90–150.

The Psalms were used as the prayer book and hymn book for the second temple (built 515 BC). An editor gave them their present number and order not later than 200 BC. Luke 24:44-45 refers to the law, the prophets, and the psalms as Scripture, though Psalms was not formally admitted to the Hebrew Bible until AD 90. The section of the Hebrew Bible containing the Psalms is called the Writings.

Divisions

Psalms is divided into five sections or books—Psalms 1–41; 42–72; 73–89; 90–106; 107–150. The first four sections each end with a doxology (see Psalm 41:13). Psalm 150 is a doxology closing both the fifth section and the book as a whole. This ancient division is apparently arbitrary and may be an attempt by an early editor to imitate the five-part division of the law.

Psalm Types
Various types of psalms are found within each of the five divisions of the book.

Laments. The laments are pleas to God to avert a threat to an individual or to the worshiping community. The individual laments (for example, Psalms 3–7) and the community laments (for example, Psalms 44; 74; 79; 80) have the following elements:

- an address to God (see Psalm 5:1)
- the lament (see Psalm 79:5)
- a petition (see Psalm 80:7)
- a confession of confidence (see Psalm 4:8)
- a vow of praise (see Psalm 13:6)

Some laments have all these elements, others only some of them. The individual lament is the most common type of psalm. Over the years, the style and form of laments changed. Some parts of this basic form were expanded (for example, the complaint against foes) and other parts were dropped (for example, the complaint against God).

Praise. The psalms of praise are prayers and songs of the community and of individuals expressing a positive relationship to God. The Hebrew words for praise include aspects of awe, adoration, and thanks. In declarative praise, the community (Psalms 124; 129; 66:8-12) and individuals (Psalms 9; 18; 22:22-31) tell of God's saving acts for the people. In descriptive praise (Psalms 65; 66; 100; 103), the psalmists praise God for being God, for God's actions as a whole. The form of the psalms of praise is not as regular as the form of the laments.

Other types. Some psalms are not readily classified. Some are hymns (songs of praise) to God's wisdom (Psalm 37), to God as king (Psalm 93), and to Zion (Psalm 87). Others, such as the songs of pilgrimage (Psalm 122), may have been part of the liturgy for a religious festival. Hymns were used for worship and festivals at home and in the temple. The so-called royal psalms praise the kings of Israel or Judah (Psalm 45).

Poetry of the Psalms

The poetry of the Psalms is the same as other Hebrew poetry. It does not have meter in the sense that European poetry does, but it does have stressed words. Each line is divided into two or more parts, and each part has stressed words. These stressed words give the poems rhythm. For example:

> *Save **me**, O God, by your **name**,*
> > *vindicate **me** by your **might**.*
> ***Hear** my **prayer**, O **God**;*
> > ***listen** to the words of my **mouth**.*
> > > *(Psalm 54:1-2)*

Scholars do not agree on how the words are transformed into metrical beats. Various systems have been proposed but none can be assumed completely correct because we still know little about Hebrew grammar and pronunciation in ancient times. The system of grammar used in the Hebrew manuscripts from which the Old Testament is translated comes not from the times of the psalmists, but from the tenth century AD.

The lines, or parts of a line, of Hebrew poetry are closely related to one another. They are parallel. There are three basic types of parallelism:

Synonymous parallelism—the second line repeats the thought of the first: "Hear this, all you peoples; / listen, all who live in this world" (Psalm 49:1).

Antithetic parallelism—the second line offers a contrast to the first: "For the LORD watches over the way of the righteous, / but the way of the wicked leads to destruction" (Psalm 1:6).

Synthetic parallelism—the second line supplements or completes the first: "I call out to the LORD, / and he answers me from his holy mountain" (Psalm 3:4).

Some psalmists grouped their lines into what we would call stanzas (some couplets, some longer). No uniform system is evident and not all psalmists used stanzas. Sometimes a stanza is indicated by the content of a poem, sometimes by a refrain.

Psalms 9; 10; 25; 34; 111; 112; 119; and 145 are acrostic poems. Each line or stanza begins with a different letter of the Hebrew alphabet. We would compose an acrostic poem with the first line beginning with A, the second line with B, the third line with C, and so on.

Theology of the Psalms

The psalms come from a variety of ages and stages in Israel's religious experience. This variety is evident in the psalm types and in the historical settings that lie behind them. Yet, the psalms tell us that those who wrote them hold certain beliefs in common. The psalmists believe in the one God who is forgiving, gracious, and willing to help people. In God they find righteousness, justice, mercy, and faithfulness. To know God is to live life at its fullest.

The psalmists tell us that God created the heavens and the earth, that God is active in nature. The psalmists see God in a particular relationship with God's people as lawgiver and as deliverer. They believe that worship is important and that the worshiping community is important to God. The psalmists assume God's power over all creation, foreseeing a time when all people will praise and worship God.

The Psalter in the Early Church

The Psalter was used in temple worship and in synagogues during the time of Jesus. Jewish Christians and the early church in general used it. Psalms is frequently quoted in the New Testament, and it provided models for New Testament hymns. (See Luke 1:46-55; 1:68-79; 2:29-32.)

The Book of Psalms has been used for hundreds of years by Jews and by Christians for both public and private expression of their faith.

LORD, our Lord, / how majestic is your name in all the earth! (8:1).

1

HYMNS OF PRAISE

DIMENSION ONE:
WHAT DOES THE BIBLE SAY?

Answer these questions by reading Psalm 8
1. The psalm talks to whom? (8:1)

> *The psalm talks to Yahweh, the Lord.*

2. What has God created? (8:3)

> *God has created the heavens, the moon, and the stars.*

3. How are human beings described in the psalm? (8:4-5)

> *Human beings are a tiny part of creation, and at the same time "a little lower than the angels."*

Answer these questions by reading Psalm 19
4. What is proclaiming God's glory in the psalm? (19:1)

> *The heavens declare God's glory.*

5. How does the psalmist describe God's law? (19:7-9)

> *God's law is perfect, trustworthy, right, radiant, pure, firm, and righteous.*

6. What must our words and thoughts be in relationship to God? (19:14)

> *They must be pleasing in God's sight.*

Answer these questions by reading Psalm 29

7. The psalm talks to whom? (29:1)

   The psalm speaks to the "heavenly beings," or the mighty ones.

8. What does the voice of God do? (29:3-9)

   The voice of God thunders, breaks cedars, makes mountains shake ("makes Lebanon leap like a calf"), brings lightning, causes earthquakes, and strips forests bare.

9. What does the psalmist ask from God? (29:11)

   The psalmist asks strength and peace for the people.

Answer these questions by reading Psalm 33

10. Who should praise God according to this psalm? (33:1)

    All righteous persons should praise God.

11. How should God be praised? (33:2-3)

    God should be praised with lyre, harp, skillful playing, a new song, and shouts for joy.

12. What does God do? (33:13-14)

    God sees "all mankind" and watches "all who live on earth."

13. What makes the psalmist glad? (33:20-21)

    Trusting in God's holy name makes the psalmist glad.

Answer these questions by reading Psalm 47

14. Who is asked to praise God? (47:1)

    All nations are to praise God.

15. Why should God be praised? (47:7)

    God should be praised because "God is the King of all the earth."

Answer these questions by reading Psalm 96

16. What kind of song does the psalmist want us to sing to God? (96:1)

    We are to sing a new song to God.

17. Why should we sing to God? (96:4-5)

    We are to sing to God because God is great and to be feared above all the gods of the nations, who are idols.

18. What should we tell the nations about God? (96:10)

    We should say that God reigns; God "will judge the peoples with equity."

Answer these questions by reading Psalm 104

19. Where do we find the clearest evidence of God's work in the world? (104:10, 14, 24)

    We must look at the creation to find evidence of God's work—the springs, the grass, the creatures.

20. How long will the psalmist praise God? (104:33)

    The psalmist will praise God as long as he lives.

DIMENSION TWO: WHAT DOES THE BIBLE MEAN?

Background Information on the Psalms

The psalms to be covered in this lesson are 8, 19, 29, 33, 47, 96, and 104. Psalms 93, 95, 97, 98, and 99 are of the same type, but are not examined in this session.

The hymns of praise are often threefold in structure. They contain a call to praise, the reasons for praise, and a vow to continue and extend praise. By indicating this type of structure, we are engaging in a scholarly approach to the psalms called *form criticism*. Study of the Bible in this way began in the early years of the twentieth century in Germany. Its founding practitioner was Hermann Gunkel, a brilliant and insightful folklorist. What he did was both simple and very important for the study of the Bible.

In a groundbreaking study of Psalms, Gunkel showed that the psalms followed literary patterns. Some were hymns of praise. Others were laments, songs of thanksgiving, and so forth. Gunkel showed us that the psalms were not only the work of the free imaginations of individual poets. They were born out of the struggles of the community of the faithful in Israel.

Gunkel wrote a history of the use of these songs in Israel's worship. From his study, whole new vistas of the early life of Israel opened up to us. To examine the forms of the psalms is to get closer to their original force and to their continuing power in the life of worship. In the psalms, we see the record of a people of faith, wrestling with life and with God's role in it. Form criticism gives us a valuable tool to discern more clearly the community that produced the great literature of Israel.

Perhaps two persistent questions concerning the psalms should be discussed here: First, who wrote the Psalms? Jewish and Christian tradition has long said that David, the second king of Israel, wrote many of the psalms. He was a famous harpist whose soothing music calmed the raging of King Saul (1 Samuel 16:23). He is said to have sung the famous lament after the deaths of Saul and Jonathan (2 Samuel 1:19-27).

The usual translation of many of the headings for the Psalms reads "A Psalm of David" (see Psalms 8 and 19, for example). In fact, the translation of these particular headings might just as easily be "A Psalm *to* David." The Hebrew could be translated either way. If this second translation is given, these psalms could be seen as dedicated to David, the patron saint of Hebrew song. Even if translated "A Psalm of David" or "David's Psalm," that is hardly proof that David wrote these psalms.

The psalms came into existence as they were needed to express community concerns in worship. Some were probably written by individuals, and some were nurtured in the worshiping community of Israel. Who wrote the psalms is a question that cannot be easily answered and is not the most important question to ask about the Book of Psalms.

The second question follows from the first: What are these headings on some of the psalms? Who wrote them? Let us look at Psalm 8 for an example. It reads "For the director of music. According to *gittith*. A psalm of David." The word translated director is not easily understood in Hebrew. It comes from a word meaning "enduring" or "eminence." Could it be a technical designation, defining a particular way of performing this psalm in the worship service? We do not know.

The second phase, "According to *gittith*," is even more mysterious. Is it a musical instrument? Is it a certain kind of musical accompaniment? Is it a reference to a particular group of musicians? Again, we do not know.

Most scholars feel that these headings were added well after the psalms originally were written. They tell us a little about when and under what circumstances the particular psalms might have been used, but they can tell us nothing about the actual writing of the Book of Psalms.

Background Information on the Hymns of Praise

The psalms of Israel and the hymns of praise did not arise from general religious feelings. No psalm of Israel was written in an ivory tower. These poems have a feeling of urgency. They were written as responses to the active presence and power of God in the real-life situations of a particular people.

People often tend to read the psalms as if they were nice, sweet poetry, addressing pleasant religious sentiments. Nothing could be further from the truth. Each psalm is the culmination of a lengthy theological struggle with basic questions about God and God's actions in the world. Let us look more closely at Psalm 96:1-3.

Sing to the LORD a new song;
    sing to the LORD, all the earth.
Sing to the LORD, praise his name;
    proclaim his salvation day after day.
Declare his glory among the nations,
    his marvelous deeds among all peoples.

This familiar religious language can dull the power locked into the words. Following the three-fold pattern of the hymns of praise, the psalmist calls on "all the earth" to sing a new song to God. But our new song is not to be senseless babble. It must have clear content. That content must be based in "his salvation day after day." Verse 3 carefully defines this as "his marvelous deeds among all peoples." In other words, God's salvation comes through God's marvelous works for all peoples.

The psalmist did not simply dream up such a lofty thought. The perception that God had actually done some marvelous work of salvation in Israel was the inspiration for the psalmist's call to praise.

We cannot be certain about the actual settings for the recital of these psalms. We can assume that all were used at one time or another in some worship setting in Israel. Psalm 96 probably was chosen by the worshiping community to praise God's power in giving victory in battle, success in harvest, or overcoming some other catastrophe.

Psalm 8. This psalm is actually a meditation on Genesis 1. What is the appropriate response to God's creation of the world and to God's creation of persons? Point out to the group the beautiful literary balance of the poem. Obviously, it begins and ends with the same phrase. In between, it speaks first about God's glory above the sky and concludes with human dominion over "all that swim the paths of the seas." In other words, God's authority stretches from above the sky to the bottom of the sea, a greater distance even than all the earth.

God's glory is spoken by the most unlikely of things—children and infants. This surprise is matched by the surprise of the human creation, which is at once tiny and yet the most significant thing in God's creation. See what other similarities to Genesis 1 you can find. Ask the group to discover some. These parallels are what give the psalm its enduring power.

Psalm 19. This psalm emphasizes the relationship between God as creator and God as law-giver. We see God as readily in God's teaching and commands as in God's physical creation. Also, the psalm helps us see the value in the Torah (Law) of God. The Law here is not a great burden from which the psalmist wants to be set free. It is more precious than gold and sweeter than honey.

Christians have often seen the word *law* through the eyes of Paul's continual plea to be free of the law. Law becomes a prison, shackles to bind persons. But Judaism never saw the Law in this way. It was quite literally God's gift of grace to the people of Israel. It was the crucial way for humanity to be "warned" (verse 11). Life needs boundaries, and God's Torah provides these.

You might ask the group what boundaries they think are essential for life. Then, too, keeping the Torah brings "great reward." This idea has been abused by many modern Christians. Many think that if you follow the Law, God will shower you with material blessings. Ask the group what they believe. What is the great reward promised here?

Psalm 29. This may be the oldest psalm in the Book of Psalms. Phrases and concepts nearly identical to those in Psalm 29 have been found in the literature of the Canaanites. This literature was found in 1929 at a place called Ugarit on the Lebanese coast of the Mediterranean Sea. These Ugaritic writings have been dated to 1500 BC.

You can sense the great age of the psalm by examining the nature symbols—thunder, lightning, wind, and earthquake. Also, we noted in the participant book the idea of a divine court of gods, ruled by Yahweh. Remind the group that monotheism, the exclusive belief in one God, was a fairly late idea in Israel's religious life. Israel was surrounded by cultures that worshiped many gods—wind, fire, storm, sun, and moon. Not until after the Exile (587–538 BC) did the writers of Israel affirm what we might call monotheism. (See Isaiah 43:10, for example.)

Have the class members discuss the psalm's unity. The "heavenly beings" begin by proclaiming the Lord's strength. The poet ends by requesting that strength from God for the people. In addition, the poet asks for peace for the people. The voice of God is the active agent in the world. The poet's voice, calling on the heavenly beings to praise, is asking us to join the praising voices as well.

Psalm 33. Verses 4 and 5 contain several key terms. The word *right* in verse 4 has the basic meaning of "straight" or "smooth." God's word is said to be not crooked, and thus not untrustworthy. The word *faithful* in verse 4 comes from the same word we say at the end of hymns and prayers, *Amen*. The word means "firmness" or "reliability." We say *Amen* because we want what we have said or sung to occur with God's help. Likewise, God's work is reliable and certain.

Two words of verse 5, *righteousness* and *justice*, are often found together, particularly among the prophets of Israel. (See Amos 5:24; Jeremiah 22:3, 15; Ezekiel 45:9.) Righteousness in the Old Testament is the fulfillment of the demands of a relationship whether with human beings or with God. It is not a passive term. One is righteous when one works to protect, restore, and help those whose rights have been taken away. Jesus is fully Hebrew in his fourth beatitude (Matthew 5:6) when he speaks of "hungering and thirsting" for righteousness, an active concern for the right. Righteousness is a particular quality of life.

Justice is the maintaining and affirming of righteousness. To be just is to be ready and willing to uphold the quality of life represented by righteousness. These two terms are among the most important in the Bible.

The last crucial term in verse 5 is *unfailing love* (*hesed* in Hebrew). This word is often used as proof of God's perpetual care for the creation. When we meet this term in the Old Testament we meet God's promise of eternal love for all of God's children. For Christians, God's unfailing love was made most evident in the gift of the son, Jesus of Nazareth.

Psalm 33 might also bring forth a discussion of God's involvement in the world (verses 8-12). How does God act with nations and people? What does the phrase, "Blessed is the nation whose God is the Lord," really mean? How do the definitions of justice and righteousness given above affect the answer to this question about the blessed nation?

Psalm 96. Notice how similar Psalm 96 is to several other hymns of praise. Compare 96:7-9 to Psalm 29:1-2, and compare 96:12-13 to 98:7-8. This similarity tells us that many of the psalms use stock and familiar phrases, phrases well known in the worshiping community. Mark Twain once said, "Familiarity breeds contempt, and children!" He may be right on both accounts, but familiarity also can be very helpful.

I have never conducted a Christian funeral without reciting the Twenty-third Psalm. Why? Its familiarity strikes deep chords in the hearts of the congregation and family. It expresses for us in certain terms the feelings we cannot easily express in our times of grief. Thus, the psalms are universal statements of praise, joy, sorrow, fear, lament, and complaint. Their universality has made them live for so long and explains why we have them even now.

You might explore with the group how the psalms were used or are about to be used in this morning's worship service. Get a bulletin and examine it together. Does the opening call to worship come from the psalms? Are any of the morning's hymns based on psalm texts? How about the responsive reading? Does your pastor ever preach from the psalms? Does your worship service itself follow a pattern familiar to you from your study of the hymns of praise? What is that form?

DIMENSION THREE: WHAT DOES THE BIBLE MEAN TO ME?

Psalm 8—GOD Is the Creator of All

A great and profound combat is raging in these hymns of praise. The psalmists are quite literally struggling for the souls of their people. Their question is, "Who created the world, and who created me?" Their answer is always, "God!" The one God, the God of justice, righteousness, and law—it is this God beside whom there is no other. As the participant book says, to praise God as sole Creator of all is to set your priorities straight. God demands absolute and ultimate loyalty, because God is the absolute and ultimately loyal creator of all.

Other religious traditions have given different answers to this great question. Some of their answers were: "Many gods had a hand in creation"; "Ra created all, but other gods create and destroy as they will"; "El creates but Baal provides." Hundreds of other answers from hundreds of other traditions could be provided. But the Hebrew answer that one God created and one God provides is a revolutionary one in human history. So if this answer is true, and if that God is really righteous, just, loyal, and loving, and if that God demands these things from the faithful, the world can be turned upside-down. This basic affirmation lies behind all the hymns of praise. This affirmation should lie behind all our relationships to God and to one another.

Psalm 19—God Is the Creator of ALL

This statement emphasizes God's universality. Once again, the psalmists are wrestling with a profound theological problem. The struggle goes on within the pages of the Bible itself. Second Kings 5 records the delightful story of Naaman, a general in the Aramean army. After he is cured of his leprosy in an unexpected way by the holy man, Elisha, he requests a load of Israelite dirt to take with him back to Aram. Why? Because he is convinced that the power of the God who saved him is somehow tied to the soil of the place of the saving. How wrong he is!

That God is universal in power and in love is an idea made clear in Amos 9:7. Israel prided herself on her chosenness. Israel was special, because God had picked her out of all the nations on earth. What Israel often forgot was that this chosenness was not for privilege but for responsibility. Thus when Amos says, "Are not you Israelites / the same to me as the Cushites?" he reminds Israel that God's concern is for all nations, and that no nation has any exclusive privilege from God at the expense of any other nation.

Jesus, most clearly in the parable of the good Samaritan (Luke 10:29-37), had this concern as a basic presupposition of his ministry. If a hated Samaritan could be "good," then anyone might be good—a militant, a pacifist—from any nation. Jesus, by stressing universality, explodes our attempts to rank people by order of merit. If God is creator of all, there can be no merit rank in God's kingdom. In God's kingdom, tax collectors abound, prostitutes and sinners gather, bad and good fill the wedding hall, and prodigal sons dance and sing. Such is the universality of God on which the hymns of praise base their songs.

To close the session you might read Psalm 96 antiphonally. Assign alternate verses to men and women, sides of the room, or leader and class.

Summarize the class session by pointing to those things you most want the class to remember about this group of psalms. And remember—praise God in all that you do!

From the rising of the sun to the place where it sets / the name of the LORD is to be praised (113:3).

HYMNS OF PRAISE

DIMENSION ONE:
WHAT DOES THE BIBLE SAY?

Answer these questions by reading Psalm 113

1. Where does the psalmist say that God is? (113:4)

    The psalmist says that God is "exalted over all the nations,"
    his glory is above the heavens.

2. Why is God worthy of praise? (113:7-9)

    God helps the helpless and the hopeless.

3. The psalm begins and ends with what words? (113:1, 9)

    "Praise the LORD."

Answer these questions by reading Psalm 114

4. What is missing from the beginning of this hymn of praise? (114:1)

    This hymn of praise has no call to worship.

5. What great events of Israel's past form the basis for this psalm? (114:1-8)

    The Exodus from Egypt and the wandering in the desert are the basis of this psalm.

6. What is missing at the end of this hymn of praise? (114:8)

    This hymn has no vow of praise.

Answer these questions by reading Psalm 121

7. How is the mood of Psalm 121 different from that of Psalm 113?

   Psalm 113 is exuberant and excited, while Psalm 121 is subdued and reflective.

8. How is God described in this psalm? (121:2, 4, 5)

   God is the ever-vigilant helper.

9. How are the endings of Psalm 121 and Psalm 113 different? (113:9 and 121:8)

   Psalm 113 ends with a shouted call to praise. Psalm 121 ends with the quiet assurance of God's continual presence.

Answer these questions by reading Psalm 135

10. Who are asked to praise God in this psalm? (135:1-2)

    The servants of the Lord who minister in the Lord's house are asked to praise God.

11. Which actions of God are praised here? (135:6-12)

    God's actions in the history of Israel from Creation to the Promised Land are praised.

12. Who are called on to praise the Lord? (135:19-20)

    The houses of Israel, Aaron, and Levi and "you who fear him" are called to praise the Lord.

Answer these questions by reading Psalm 145

13. How does the psalmist describe God's greatness? (145:3)

    God's greatness is unfathomable.

14. How is God described in this psalm? (145:8)

    The Lord is gracious, compassionate, slow to anger, and rich in love.

15. In whom is God especially interested? (145:14)

    God is especially interested in those who fall and who are bowed down.

Answer these questions by reading Psalm 146

16. How long will the psalmist praise God? (146:2)

The psalmist will praise God as long as he lives.

17. Why should we not trust in princes? (146:3-4)

The plans of princes die with their deaths and so come to nothing.

18. To whom does God show special care? (146:7-9)

God shows special care for the oppressed, hungry, prisoners, blind, bowed down, foreigner, fatherless, and widowed.

Answer these questions by reading Psalm 150

19. Where should God be praised? (150:1)

God should be praised in the sanctuary and in God's mighty heavens.

20. Why should God be praised? (150:2)

God should be praised for acts of power and surpassing greatness.

21. How should God be praised? (150:3-5)

God should be praised with all musical instruments "and dancing."

22. Who should praise God? (150:6)

Everything that breathes should praise God.

DIMENSION TWO:
WHAT DOES THE BIBLE MEAN?

The psalms we will examine in more detail in this lesson are Psalms 113, 114, 121, 135, 145, 146, and 150. Psalms 115, 117, 134, 147, 148, and 149 are psalms of the same type, but will not be studied in this session.

Psalm 113. We examined the contrasting language of Psalm 8 in Lesson 1. We need to do the same for this psalm. The imagery of this song is spatial throughout. That is, the locations of the actors and actresses of the poem are crucial for its proper understanding.

Verse 3 begins the imagery when it defines the appropriate time to praise God as "the rising of the sun to the place where it sets." From low to high to low defines the movement within the psalm. So, God is first introduced as "exalted over all the nations" (verse 4). God's exalted position transcends all human groups. But God is even higher than that! God's glory is far above the sky. Even above the highest thing a human eye can see, so is God's glory, God's presence, God's power. From this lofty seat God "stoops down to look" (verse 6) upon the sky, not to mention the earth.

The psalm's spatial imagery now shifts dramatically. The infinitely lofty God "raises . . . and lifts" (verse 7). And those God raises and lifts are the lowest members of society, the poor and the needy. The latter word, *needy*, is used about forty times in the Old Testament, nearly always in a material sense. (See Psalms 109:16; 72:12; 82:4.) The word poor is directly the opposite of *rich*. The poor are persons whose prosperity and social status have been reduced. They are suspect in the eyes of the society, not unlike the poor of our own communities. These persons, says the psalmist, will be raised by God to sit "with princes." In other words, the inequities of economic society will be changed by the power of God.

The third example is that of the childless woman becoming a mother. How many stories of both the Old and New Testaments rest on this problem! Sarai, Rebekah, Rachel, Hannah, and Elizabeth were all childless women who eventually had children. In ancient Israel, motherhood was highly prized and a woman's fulfillment was thought to come in her motherhood. Obviously, much of that feeling has carried over into our own lives. This fact has often led to the denigration of childless women and childless couples. But in the small society of Israel, large families were God's blessings, and the women always had the central role to play. So the psalmist asserts that it is the most high God who grants the childless woman a child. And for that great deed, God is worthy of praise.

Thus, the psalm begins with the command to praise God. Then that God is described as lofty beyond description, but also as the God who reaches down to lift the most lowly. And the command to praise is repeated with renewed force. This God is truly worthy of resounding praise.

Psalm 114. This psalm is a marvelous example of how the traditions of Israel were kept alive by the worshiping community. This simple recital of God's past great deeds served to educate the community and to retell long-ago acts. These acts are the work of a God who is still acting even as the psalmist writes and as the worshiper repeats the writing aloud.

A narrative psalm of praise, this psalm begins very much like the Bible itself. An alternative reading of Genesis 1:1, "When God began to create," is a more appropriate translation of the Hebrew text than the traditional "In the beginning." So here we read, "When Israel came out of Egypt."

The psalmist sets the historical context of the narrative immediately. Verse 1 begins to interpret the event of the Exodus for the worshiper to celebrate. "When Israel came out of Egypt," Israel became God's "holy thing" and "kingdom" (a literal rendering for the words *sanctuary* and *dominion*). The psalmist explains that in the Exodus event God created Israel as a "holy kingdom."

Or one might say, on the west bank of the sea, one finds a group of terrified slaves; on the east bank, there stands a nation.

The next verse joins together two traditions about famous bodies of water. The drowning of the Egyptians in the Red Sea and the safe passage of the Israelites through that same sea (Exodus 14) are parts of a familiar incident. Note that the old tradition that this is the Red Sea is not supported by the Hebrew text that clearly calls the spot "the sea of reeds" (see footnote to Exodus 13:18). The eastern end of the Nile delta region is virtually covered with reeds. This event is to be celebrated, not proved.

The event at the Jordan River is a similar tradition. Joshua 3:14-17 says the Jordan River ceases to flow, allowing the Israelites to cross on dry ground. Both events are described and then affirmed as celebrations of God's power and presence.

Then, in Psalm 114:5-6 these great events of the past, well known to all Israelites, are expanded into huge cataclysms of the earth. The sea "fled"; the Jordan "turned back"; the mountains "leaped like rams." The worshiper is brought into the past and then pulled into the present with a God who acts.

The psalm ends with another reference to a past event. The story of God's miraculous provision of water in the desert is found in Exodus 17:6 and Numbers 20:11. But God's past actions are not confined to the past. Indeed, they become for this psalmist assurances of God's continuing action in the present. To recite this psalm is itself to praise God.

Psalm 121. The short title of this psalm may give us a clue as to its use in Israel. Beginning with Psalm 120, the next fifteen psalms have the same heading, translated as "a song of ascents." These psalms probably were used often by pilgrims on feast journeys to the great holy shrines of ancient Israel, most especially Jerusalem. In Psalm 121, the pilgrim may raise the issue and question of the first verse, while a priest or cultic official may respond with the remainder of the psalm. Seen with this background, Psalm 121 becomes a psalm of assurance and praise. The question of verse 1 is answered by the praise of the God who "watches," a God forever awake and alert on behalf of those who worship.

The word *watches* is used with almost monotonous repetition. Hebrew style indicates that repetition is the way to emphasize an idea. You and I would choose synonyms to do the same thing; the Hebrew author repeats. Passages that sound uninteresting to our ears possess repetitive power to the Hebrews. To judge the Bible only by our canons of literary style is to make a serious error. When one finishes this psalm of praise, one is convinced that God watches over all of life, forever. And this was the author's intent.

Psalm 135. This hymn is directed toward the priests in Israel. This fact is seen clearly in verses 1-2 and verses 19-20. In other words, the address to the priests frames the entire poem.

The role of the priests in ancient Israel is a complex subject. In a famous passage, God chose Israel to be "a kingdom of priests and a holy nation" (Exodus 19:6). The phrase is better translated "a kingdom of priests, that is a holy nation." Israel is called to be a holy nation in imitation of God who is holy. Thus, the first role of the organized priesthood is to represent the holy nation. In all public and national worship, the priests represent the people.

But the roles of the priests were not only practical. They were also moral and spiritual. Because any nation can only be more or less holy, the priest could be uniquely holy and sanctified. This, of course, was and is the ideal. Not all priests were holy persons. (See, for example, the story of Hophni and Phinehas, the corrupt, priestly sons of Eli in 1 Samuel 2:12-17.) But the priestly office was created in part to represent the whole people of God.

Three types of priests served in the priesthood. The lowest order of priests were the Levites, who served in the sanctuary (see Psalm 135:1-2). Above them were the sons of Aaron, who were specifically consecrated as priests. They alone could function in the worship services at the altar. Finally, there was the high priest, who alone could enter the most sacred place of the sanctuary, the Most Holy Place.

When Psalm 135:19-20 calls for both Aaronites and Levites to "praise the LORD," it includes all the temple personnel in the summons. All who serve in the sanctuary must take special care to be holy and to praise and bless God with correct behavior. (See the story of Nadab and Abihu in Leviticus 10:1-3.)

Psalm 135 contains a historical summary of God's past actions in verses 6-12. It differs from Psalm 121 at several points. First, it begins the summary with the language of the creation of the world. The words *heavens*, *earth*, *seas*, and *depths* all refer to the opening verses of Genesis 1. But the creator God does not then cease to act. God, in verse 7, "brings clouds up from the ends of the earth, makes lightning for the rain, brings wind from its chambers" (my translation). The God who forms the earth and sky still controls their activities.

And then the psalmist moves into history with the recital of events. The author paints in quick strokes the tenth plague of Egypt (verses 8-9); the defeat of the Amorite kings, Sihon and Og (verses 10-11; see Numbers 21:21-35); and the gift of the Promised Land (verse 12).

Thus, the psalmist has moved from the creation of the world to the gift of Israel's Promised Land. For all that God is to be praised. And it is the special responsibility of the priests and Levites to represent Israel in that praise and to lead them to their own praise.

Psalm 145. As suggested in the participant book, this poem is an acrostic one. Each line begins with another letter of the Hebrew alphabet in sequential order. Here, however, for some reason we cannot discern, the line beginning with the letter *nun* has fallen out. But in the Septuagint, a Greek translation done in the third century BC, the translator has included a line that does begin with *nun*. He either supplied a line on his own to complete the form, or he had a Hebrew manuscript that included such a line. We can probably never know.

Other alphabetic acrostic psalms include Psalms 9–10, 25, 34, 111, and 112. Another, the lengthy Psalm 119, is written so that blocks of eight lines begin with each successive Hebrew letter making it 176 lines long. A highly artificial way to write a poem, this style severely limits the word choice. A closer look at Psalm 145 reveals a long series of stock religious phrases, many of which come from other parts of the Old Testament.

I have tried several times to translate one of these psalms from Hebrew to English, maintaining the alphabetic sequence. I found it impossible. We should ask why nine of the psalms from the collection were written this way. Primarily, we can be sure, it was a memory game, very helpful in religious education for priests and people. Then, too, the inevitable patterning has its own kind of power. Finally, it was probably just fun to do!

Two other items are of special note in this psalm. Psalm 145:8 quotes one of the great descriptions of God in the Bible. The most significant use of this phrase comes from Exodus 34:6. At that point, Moses has gone back up the mountain of Sinai to receive a second time the tablets of the commandments. The first time he smashed the set in a rage (see Exodus 32). The tablets were recut, but then Moses made an unprecedented request to God. He asked God to "teach me your ways" (Exodus 33:13). And so God passed in front of Moses and revealed those ways with the phrase found in Psalm 145:8. The part about punishing "the children and their children for the sin of the parents to the third and fourth generation" is missing here. (See Exodus 34:6-7.) When the wayward prophet Jonah quotes this phrase (Jonah 4:2), he, too, leaves out the punishment part of the saying. The reason for this omission in this psalm and in Jonah seems clear. Both authors want to emphasize and highlight the tremendous grace and compassion of God. For the psalmist, this is why God is worthy of praise.

The other item of interest in Psalm 145 is the tension between God's special care for the powerless (145:14) and God's care for all (145:15). (For a discussion of this topic, see Dimension Three in the participant book.) The Bible's message here walks on a razor's edge. God has chosen Israel, but for a universal mission. The tension between uniqueness and universality is always in evidence. So, too, God loves all, but has special concern for those who have special needs. Liberation theologies often proclaim, "God is on the side of the poor." And they are right in so saying. But God is on the side of humanity, both oppressed and oppressor. The Bible's tension remains between God's love for all and God's special love for the powerless.

Psalm 146. Two concerns are of interest in Psalm 146. The contrast is drawn between earthly leaders, the princes whose power is limited by inevitable death, and God who lives forever. This comment about the inadequacy of humanity and the transitory nature of human life reminds us of Psalm 144:3-4.

The second concern is related to the first. The princes of the world have apparently created a society that is in shambles. Oppression, hunger, prisoners, widows, fatherless, and general wickedness characterize the world of the princes. But God has a better idea. God sets about correcting the disasters of the princes by freeing the prisoners; feeding the hungry; and aiding the foreigner, widow, and fatherless. As suggested, God is uniquely concerned with those and calls us all to be equally concerned. One could readily say that a society, as much as an individual, is judged in the sight of God by its treatment of these.

Psalm 150. No more fitting psalm than this one could be found to close the Book of Psalms. It begins and ends with the familiar command to "Praise the LORD." God is to be praised everywhere, both inside the sanctuary and throughout God's mighty heavens. The Hebrew word, here translated heavens, is used in Genesis 1:6 when God creates the expanse to divide the primeval waters. It more literally means a "beaten-out thing" or "a bowl." Another translation of the word as vault captures the shape very well. The "vault of the sky" encloses the entire inhabited world. Inside this vault, where you and I live, we are called to praise just as certainly as we are called to praise inside our vaulted sanctuaries.

All instruments are summoned to the praise of God. The trumpet is the *shofar*, most primitively a ram's horn, but later horns of the ibex and antelope were used. The shofar was used to signal the people in war and in peace as well as in worship. Synagogues still use a ram's horn on festal occasions to remind them of how God substituted a ram when Abraham was willing to sacrifice Isaac (see Genesis 22).

The word translated harp, *nēbel*, is sometimes rendered as lute. Psalm 33:2 speaks of a *nēbel* with ten strings. We can be certain it was a stringed instrument of some kind. The harp definitely was an upright stringed instrument. Egyptian harps as old as 3,500 years were found in tombs of the pharaohs. The word *strings* is a general term, encompassing harps and lyres.

The list of instruments includes those usually set aside for either secular or sacred use. The trumpet, lyre, and harp are priestly instruments, while the pipe is a secular one. But in Psalm 150 all instruments are called into the service of God's praise.

DIMENSION THREE: WHAT DOES THE BIBLE MEAN TO ME?

Psalm 121—Where Can I See God at Work Today?

This question of God's activity in the world today is a difficult one. It could easily be documented that the growth of churches that emphasize experiential religion (active worship services, speaking in tongues, healing services) is directly attributable to the need in all of us for proof. If God is active in the world, we are eager to see signs.

Nothing is inherently wrong in the desire for proof, but it can cause problems. For example, if my faith in God is based on the constant recurrence of signs and wonders, is that faith really in God, or is it in the signs and wonders? When water gushed from the rock in Exodus 17, it is remembered negatively as a time when Israel was testing God. Surely, not all Christians who claim special proof of God's presence in their lives are putting God to the test. But the danger is there.

Ask the class members about God's presence in their lives. Do they feel that presence? If so, how? If not, do they feel a void there? Ask those who do feel that presence to explain how they feel it. What does Jesus' statement to doubting Thomas (John 20:24-29) mean for this problem?

Psalms 113:7-9; 145:14; 146:7-9—God Is the God of the Powerless

Jose Miranda, a Latin American theologian of liberation, writes in *Marx and the Bible* about the dilemma between justice and worship. He says this dilemma occurs when people who are suffering injustice worship and pray without God as their object. To know God is to do justice and compassion and right to the needy.

Have the class members discuss Miranda's idea in the light of God's universal concern for the world. Do you agree with Miranda? Why or why not? What are the implications of what he says?

Close this session with an antiphonal reading (groups of persons reading alternating lines of the psalm) of Psalm 150.

*L*ORD, *who may dwell in your sacred tent? / Who may live on your holy mountain? (15:1).*

SONGS OF ZION

DIMENSION ONE:
WHAT DOES THE BIBLE SAY?

Answer these questions by reading Psalm 15

1. What does the psalmist mean by "your sacred tent"? (15:1)

   "Your sacred tent" is another name for God's holy mountain (Zion).

2. How does one gain entrance to the holy mountain? (15:2-5)

   To get to God's holy mountain one must walk blamelessly, do what is righteous, speak the truth, do no wrong to a neighbor, honor those who fear God, keep oaths, charge no interest on a loan, and accept no bribe.

Answer these questions by reading Psalm 24

3. What belongs to the Lord? (24:1)

   The earth and everything in it belongs to God.

4. Who is able to stand in God's holy place? (24:4)

   Whoever has clean hands and a pure heart can stand in the holy place.

5. Who is the King of glory? (24:8, 10)

   The Lord, strong and mighty in battle, the Lord Almighty is the King of glory.

Answer these questions by reading Psalm 46

6. How can we survive in a tumultuous world? (46:1-3)

   We must trust in God, our refuge and strength.

7. Where does God dwell? (46:4)

God dwells in the city of God (Zion).

8. What are the works of the Lord? (46:9)

God stops wars by destroying the weapons that wage them.

Answer these questions by reading Psalm 48

9. Why is God to be praised? (48:1-8)

God defeated the armies of those who would destroy the city of God.

10. What is the task given to each reader of the psalm? (48:12-14)

Each reader is to understand and appreciate Zion (Jerusalem) and tell the next generation about the God who made and sustains it.

Answer these questions by reading Psalm 76

11. What is "Salem" in this psalm? (76:2)

"Salem" is a short form of Jerusalem (Zion).

12. What is God's great work? (76:3, 5-6, 9)

God's great work is to destroy the means of war.

13. What does God do to the rulers and kings of the earth? (76:12)

God breaks their spirit and is fearsome to them.

Answer these questions by reading Psalm 84

14. Where is God's dwelling place? (84:7)

God dwells in Zion.

15. How is God described in this psalm? (84:2, 3, 7, 11)

God is the living God, king, God in Zion, sun and shield.

Answer these questions by reading Psalm 122

16. What is Jerusalem's role in this psalm? (122:3-4)

Jerusalem is a focal point to unite the tribes of the Lord (Israel).

17. Is Jerusalem the main concern of the psalm? (122:9)

No. Jerusalem should be preserved for the sake of the house of God, the temple.

DIMENSION TWO:
WHAT DOES THE BIBLE MEAN?

The psalms covered in this lesson are Psalms 15, 24, 46, 48, 76, 84, and 122. Psalms 87 and 132 are psalms of the same type, but are not considered in this session.

The psalms of Zion are collected around the subject of Zion as God's sacred place, God's holy mountain. (Technically, hills and mountains are defined now by a differentiation in height, but this designation is not the issue in these psalms. The Temple Mount, for example, is on a hill.) The oldest meaning of the word *Zion* is the fortified hill of pre-Israelite Jerusalem. The mention of Zion in 2 Samuel 5:6-10 probably refers to that fortified area on top of the hill near the Kidron Valley. The name *Jerusalem* referred to the whole area, including small towns and villages in the area as well as the hill of Zion.

When the ark of the LORD (referred to also as "the ark of the covenant"), brought by David to Jerusalem (see 2 Samuel 6), is transferred to Solomon's temple, the name *Zion* was itself transferred to the temple area. (See for example, Psalms 2:6; 132:13.) In later poetry and in prophetic writings, *Zion* equals Jerusalem as God's religious capital, the object of God's grace or punishment. (See Isaiah 28:16; see also Romans 9:33.)

Still another use of *Zion* is as a synonym for the people of Jerusalem. Phrases such as "sons of Zion" or "daughters of Zion" are used to describe men and women who receive God's mercy or are victims of God's wrath. (See Psalm 97:8; Isaiah 1:27; Joel 2:23.)

These psalms refer to this Zion tradition at various stages of the tradition. Zion becomes for the Israelites much more than a place. It shines as a beacon light of hope for the future of God in their lives.

Psalm 15:1. The parallelism of "sacred tent" and "holy mountain" indicates the shifting significance of the traditions of Zion. The basic unit in any psalm is the verse of two lines, usually related to one another in some sort of parallel way. In 15:1, the psalmist wants us to parallel "sacred tent" of line 1 with "holy mountain" of line 2. The sacred tent reminds us of the desert days when the Israelites worshiped God in a portable sanctuary, the tent of meeting. (See Exodus 33:7-11; Numbers 2:2.)

Exodus 33:7-11 gives the clearest indication of the function of the tent of meeting. The tent was portable and was pitched outside the camp. It then probably served as a tribal meeting hall as well as a place of revelation. This tent seems to represent the awesome mystery and transcendence of God who descends to it to speak to Moses. Just as in those old days, when God's power was revealed in the tent, now Zion is the place to go to find God. The pilgrims of the psalms thus go to Zion.

Psalm 15:2-5. Here the stipulations for entrance into Zion are listed. Ten stipulations, a typically Hebrew number of laws, are listed. The list begins with the general requirements to walk blamelessly, do right, and speak the truth. Then the next five are slightly more specific and refer to human relations of a verbal kind (no slander, no slur, honor, and keep oaths). Finally, the last two are very specific commands that are examples of the others. This technique of moving from the general to the more specific to the quite specific emphasizes the fact that "doing right" is not a general act but a quite specific one.

A few more words should be said about the specific concerns of verse 5. The first line of verse 5 does not prohibit interest on loans in general, only loans to the poor. On examining Leviticus 25:35-37, we discover that the prohibition against lending money at interest to a "fellow Israelite" who becomes poor is based on the responsibility for his livelihood. He needs to be able to live "among you." The last line of the psalm is probably a reference to this very passage in Leviticus.

He or she who does all these things in 15:2-5 "will never be shaken." In Leviticus 25:35, the phrase "help them" is literally "they will be moved by you." Thus, the psalmist ties your responsibility to maintain the unfortunate brother or sister to your own maintenance in the sight of God. Also, as the second line of verse 5 notes, taking a bribe is unacceptable behavior to God, especially a bribe at the expense of the poor (see Exodus 23:8).

Psalm 24. This psalm may provide one of the clearest pictures of an ancient Israelite festival available to us. Let us call it the festival of God's kingship. Verses 1-2 are a short hymn to the Creator and probably would be uttered as the procession reached the outside of the temple gates. The questions in verse 3 would be asked by the leader of the procession. Verses 4-5 would be the response of the gatekeeper. Verse 6 would again be the procession leader, assuring the gatekeeper that all those who seek admittance have fulfilled the requirements. Verses 7-10 form the request from the procession of pilgrims to open the gates to allow the entry of the King of glory, perhaps symbolized in the ark of the Lord. Thus, we have here an ancient responsive reading.

A further look at the liturgy demonstrates a theological unity. God demonstrates divine glory in the creation of the world (verses 1-2). God's worshipers, if they are worthy of this great God, must meet certain stipulations that they do meet (verses 3-6). Then worshipers and God enter the sanctuary with great rejoicing (verses 7-10).

One can hardly prove that this scene I have constructed is how the psalm was used. It does provide a plausible background for the psalm and suggests the power of the psalm's use over time in the liturgy of Israel.

Psalm 46. This psalm celebrates God's ultimate victory over the nations. The victory will most easily be recognized in the safety of the Holy City of Zion. The psalmist refers to a long-ago victory of God over the forces of the sea at the creation of the world (verses 2-3). Many stories of creation exist in the ancient Near East, and most of them talk about a great combat between two warring deities. Both Babylonian and Canaanite stories reflect this idea.

Israel knew these stories and incorporated them into its images of God's creation of the world. One can see references to these old combat myths in Isaiah 51:9, Job 38:8, and Ezekiel 26:19. The Israelites did not believe those old mythologies. They simply borrowed them to make more colorful and powerful statements of God's control over the universe.

Next, to contrast with this violent defeat of the ancient waters, the psalmist presents a picture of the river of Jerusalem (verse 4). This gentle stream of God now safeguards Jerusalem and helps make it holy. Other places refer to this Jerusalem river. In Isaiah 33:21, the stream will be broad, but no warships will be allowed, an oblique reference to the reign of peace willed by God. In Ezekiel 47:1-2, the river is described as flowing "from under the threshold of the temple," making the waters of the Dead Sea fresh, and providing moisture for the growing of magic trees that bear monthly fruit for food and for healing. Zechariah 14:8 mentions this river, and Revelation 22:1-2 reiterates the fruit tree image of Ezekiel. This river image, and all the different uses of it, adds to the picture of God's will for peace and prosperity for the people who worship God.

The psalmist goes on to describe God's presence in the temple, God's victory over all the peoples of earth, God's subjugation of all evil powers, and the establishment of universal peace. The chief subject of the psalm is that the people have an unshakable trust in God.

Psalm 48. As in Psalm 46, this psalm celebrates a great victory of God over some enemy, assembled around the walls of Jerusalem. God has achieved the great victory in defense of the sacred Zion. Verses 4-7 describe the great victory. Early commentators used to look for some specific historical victory at Jerusalem to discover the meaning of this passage. They pointed, for example, to the failure of Sennacherib, king of Assyria, to pierce the walls of Jerusalem in 701 BC. (See 2 Kings 19:32-37.)

But to look for an exact historical reference is to miss the power of the psalm completely. We do not worship God and praise God because of one defeat of our enemies in the past. We worship God because we are convinced of God's continuous victory over our enemies in the present and in the future. In this regard, verse 8 is crucial. "Just exactly as we have heard, so we have seen" (my translation). The psalmist makes a very important point. We can always hear about God from others, but unless we see and are convinced that God acts for us, we will not believe what we hear. One of the most important functions of the psalms is to make God's continuous activity real in the lives of the present worshipers. Thus are psalms new for each new generation of worshipers.

Psalm 48:12-14. These verses seem to describe the end of a ritual practice. The worshipers are asked to "walk about Zion." This going around the sacred place is reminiscent of the famous walk around the *Kaabah*, the black stone in the center of the sacred mosque in Mecca, the holiest city of Islam. Each year hundreds of thousands of Muslim pilgrims trek to Mecca and walk around the black stone as part of the pilgrimage ritual. Surely, Psalm 48:12 is a forerunner of such a ritual. After the walk is over, the worshipers are commanded to go out and tell others what they have seen and experienced. Verse 14 is a benediction ending the worship.

Psalm 76. As in Psalm 48, we hear again about God's destruction of past enemies (verses 5-6). In this psalm, we are urged to celebrate God's continuous defeat of enemies and the final defeat of all divine foes.

Psalm 76:2. Only here and in Genesis 14:18 in all the Hebrew Bible does the short form, *Salem*, appear for "Jerusalem." The word itself is a form of the famous word for peace, *shalom*, or better translated *unity, wholeness.*

Psalm 76:3-6. When one reads these words, one inevitably thinks of the defeat of the Egyptians by God at the Red Sea, described in Exodus 14–15. (Compare verse 6 with Exodus 15:1.) But again, we should not limit our understanding of these verses to one historical occasion. The defeat at the sea is used merely as a poetic example to describe God's ultimate victory on behalf of the oppressed of the earth.

Psalm 76:7-9. This psalm possibly was sung at a yearly festival of the enthronement of God. If this was the case, the king probably played the role of God in a great festival drama. In verse 2, the king, on behalf of God, takes the throne in Salem. After the enthronement of God, God utters judgment from the heavens. This judgment stills the enemies, and their weapons of war are destroyed. The psalmist does not have in mind any one defeat in history nor the final defeat of all enemies at the end of time. The congregation worshiping on that very day is called to celebrate God's continuous victory. Only in this way can ancient psalms retain their freshness and power for each generation.

Psalm 84. *A German Requiem*, by Johannes Brahms, includes words from Psalm 84:1-2. The music wonderfully captures the longing to come to the sacred place and worship God. You might get a recording and play this chorus for your group. (Check with your local library.) The entire poem is structured around the journey to Jerusalem and is a song of pilgrimage.

Psalm 84:1-2. The pilgrims, before they begin the journey, affirm their ardent desire to make the trip. The word translated soul in verse 2 is the word *nefesh* in Hebrew, The word *nefesh* more literally means "all that I am, my true being," because the Israelites did not believe in a separation of spirit and body. Thus, every part of the pilgrim longs for the house of God.

Psalm 84:3-4. God's house encompasses even the birds of the air. The lowliest of creatures has a place in God's house, and creatures who find a home there are blessed.

Psalm 84:5-7. Now pilgrims, whose hearts have pathways leading to God, are also called blessed. As they progress toward Jerusalem, they go through dangerous valleys, but their faith and joy in God sustains them. The word *Baka* may be a misspelling for a similar word that means "weeping." The expectation of seeing the God of gods in Zion maintains the joy of the journey.

Psalm 84:10. The greatness of God's court is affirmed. You might compare this psalm with Psalms 15 and 14. Those psalms emphasize the requirements for entering the sacred place of God. Here, the earnest pilgrims do not dwell on those requirements. Rather, they are most concerned just with getting there and basking in God's favor.

Psalm 122. In this pilgrim song, the pilgrims appear to have arrived in Jerusalem. They have examined the city and have admired it for its unity and for the unity it symbolizes for them and for the tribes of Israel as a whole.

DIMENSION THREE:
WHAT DOES THE BIBLE MEAN TO ME?

Psalm 15—What Does the Lord Require of Me?

In some religious circles, some well-meaning Christians claim that God's demands are limited to concerns of individual morality. "All right with God" means for them that their souls have been saved. They do not use profanity, their clothes are pressed, and their hair is cut. Some go further to claim that God has saved them and they need never fear again. Other Christians say that God's deepest concerns are for the poor and the outcast. Any society that does not care most particularly for the least of the sisters and brothers is a society far from God, no matter what the size of their churches or the fervor of their worship. Both of these groups are right together, but not separately. Unless these two sides can draw together, the power of the gospel can never be heard.

One can never get right with God without getting right with the society one lives in. On the other hand, no one can serve the cause of societal justice for very long without a deep personal commitment to God. Both Psalm 15, with its sharp societal demands, and Psalm 121, studied in the last lesson, with its meditative, personal view of God's presence, must be affirmed to capture the wholeness of God's demands for you and me.

The dangers of adhering strictly to either view are profound. Loving God in splendid isolation, praying and praising God without actions of justice, lead to individualism and then to cynicism. Individualism is the great blasphemy of our time, because when the pronouns are all first-person, giving becomes difficult, if not impossible. Jesus knew this danger all too well. When he describes the high cost of discipleship, he warns that the first step is always self-denial (Mark 8:34). If I cannot deny myself, that is, if I cannot move myself out of the very center of creation, I inevitably see the world as one that revolves around me and my needs.

This attitude leads to cynicism. Many feel that "I ain't much, but I'm all I've got." If we are all we have, then we have very little at all! If I'm all I've got, we all are in real trouble! The result of such a belief is cynicism of a profound kind. I'm all there is; I'm not much; that's it! Strict individualism always leads to cynicism. If the only future I have is more of me, then there can be no eternal significance to my life. The road beyond self comes in self-denial and in shouldering a cross, to move to Jesus' step 2 of real discipleship.

The danger of the other pole is equally great. If I only act and do in society without a well of personal faith to draw upon, my impetus to action is soon dried up. One should "never weary in well-doing" (see Galatians 6:9), but without deep reasons for the doing, it soon loses its purpose. Where are many of my activist friends of the sixties? The Vietnam War galvanized them into action. But with the waning of the fighting and the United States' involvement, the fervor left. Where is the same effort against hunger and homelessness? Only those with a deep commitment to something larger than themselves and their needs can persist in the hard causes of justice.

What then does the Lord require of you? Micah 6:8, from which this famous quotation comes, puts it very well. Allow my translation to clarify the issue.

> *God has told you, humanity, what is good,*
> *What Yahweh seeks from you.*
> *Nothing but the doing of justice, the loving*
> *of kindness, and carefully walking with your God.*

Kindness and justice can only be maintained in life when one continues to work carefully with God. Let us then unite the two so often divided—devotion to God and devotion to justice. Only then will we know what God requires of us.

Ask the class members these questions. Is the Micah 6:8 passage helpful to you? What do you think the Lord requires of you?

Jerusalem: What's in It for Me?

Jerusalem has become, in the songs of Zion, more than just a place. For the psalmists, Jerusalem was a living symbol of God's will for eternal peace and justice. Explore with the group the crucial importance of symbols for their lives.

Ask them what their most important symbols are. Some answers they might give are the cross, the fish, the American flag, or perhaps a company symbol. Help them explore why symbols are important. What is the value of symbols?

In a world that still sees bitter fighting and animosity between nations, leaving a wake of poverty, despair, and orphaned children, what can a symbol of peace be and mean?

In a sense, Jerusalem becomes to some psalmists at least the peace symbol of ancient Israel. The psalmists who wrote Psalms 48 and 76 certainly used it in this way. Their culture was no less riddled with war and hostility than our own. But Jerusalem became for them the place of rest and safety, the Holy City of peace and justice. Do you have one symbol that encompasses your life, one that gives you ultimate meaning? Could you share it with the group?

Our two concerns for this lesson dovetail at this point. As we perceive more specifically what the Lord requires of us, we will choose appropriate symbols to help us strive toward that goal of being in God's will.

You might close the session by listing the symbols chosen by the members and letting them express why these symbols were theirs.

*The king rejoices in your strength, L*ORD*. / How great is his joy in the victories you give! (21:1).*

ROYAL PSALMS

DIMENSION ONE:
WHAT DOES THE BIBLE SAY?

Answer these questions by reading Psalm 2

1. Who stands with the Lord against the kings of the earth? (2:2)

    The Lord's "anointed" stands with the Lord.

2. What will the Lord do for "his anointed"? (2:8-9)

    The Lord will make the nations of the earth the king's/anointed's heritage and possession.

3. What should all earthly rulers do? (2:11)

    They should serve the Lord with fear and celebrate with trembling.

Answer these questions by reading Psalm 18

4. How does the psalmist describe his difficulty to God? (18:4-5)

    The psalmist is surrounded by cords of death, torrents of destruction, and cords of the grave (Sheol).

5. How is God described in the psalm? (18:2, 8-15)

    God is a rock, fortress, and deliverer. Also God has smoke rising "from his nostrils" and consuming fire coming "from his mouth." God scattered the enemies with "great bolts of lightning."

6. Who is speaking in the psalm? (18:50)

    The Davidic king of Israel is the speaker in this psalm.

Answer these questions by reading Psalm 20

7. Who is the "you" of verse 1? (20:1, 6)

 > *The "you" of verse 1 is the Lord's anointed, the king.*

8. In what should we trust? (20:7)

 > *We should trust in the name of the Lord our God.*

Answer these questions by reading Psalm 21

9. Why should the king trust in the Lord? (21:7)

 > *Because of the Lord's unfailing love, the king should trust so "he will not be shaken."*

10. Whose strength is exalted in the poem, God's or the king's? (21:13)

 > *God's strength is exalted.*

Answer these questions by reading Psalm 45

11. Who is the psalmist here? (45:1)

 > *The psalmist is a skillful writer (scribe) in the royal court of the king.*

12. How is the king described in the psalm? (45:2, 5)

 > *The king is described as the most excellent of men and a great warrior, victorious over his enemies.*

Answer these questions by reading Psalm 72

13. What is the chief role of the king in Israel? (72:2)

 > *He is to judge the people with righteousness and the afflicted with justice.*

14. Why is it hoped that the king will endure "as long as the sun"? (72:5, 12-14)

 > *The king delivers the needy, the afflicted, the weak, and the oppressed.*

15. What is the result of a righteous king? (72:1, 8-11, 16)
    Distant kings will honor and serve him, and his own land will prosper with abundant grain and other crops.

Answer these questions by reading Psalm 89

16. Why is God described as "greatly feared" and "awesome"? (89:7, 9-13)
    God is described this way because God has created the world and is a powerful ruler over it.

17. Who anoints the kings of Israel? (89:20)
    God anoints the kings of Israel.

18. How long will David's throne last? (89:29)
    His throne will last "as long as the heavens endure."

Answer these questions by reading Psalm 110

19. What will God do for "my Lord"? (110:1)
    God will defeat my Lord's enemies.

20. Who is Melchizedek? (110:4)
    Melchizedek is the priest that the king must imitate.

DIMENSION TWO:
WHAT DOES THE BIBLE MEAN?

The psalms covered in this lesson are Psalms 2, 18, 20, 21, 45, 72, 89, and 110. Psalms 101 and 144 are of the same type, but will not be considered in this lesson.

The royal psalms provide a fascinating glimpse into the world of ancient Israelite kingship and its festivals. We have learned the shape of the coronation ritual of the kings of Israel from First and Second Kings. When Solomon became king at the death of David, his father, the steps of his ascension to the throne are clearly described (see 1 Kings 1:33-35). He first rides on the king's sacred mule and then is actually anointed by the chief priest and the king's prophet, presumably in the temple. The festival then moved to the king's palace. After the temple ceremony, the new king is taken to the palace where he sits upon the throne. (See the story of Jehoiada, the priest, taking the throne from Athaliah in 2 Kings 11:19-20.) That is the basic outline of the festival.

Within the royal psalms other details can be seen and identified. We will examine some of these details as we look more carefully at the psalms themselves.

Psalm 2:1-6. In this coronation hymn, we can trace the outlines of the ritual. Verses 1-3 proclaim the foolishness and evil of all the enemies of God and king. All plots and schemes will be foiled by God who has uniquely chosen the ruler. To counter the plots, God laughs in the heavens (verses 4-5) and reacts to their muttering together with a clear proclamation (verse 6), "I have installed my king / on Zion, my holy mountain."

For an early Christian interpretation of verses 1-3, see Acts 4:25-29. There the plotting foreign rulers are Herod and Pilate and the anointed one of God is Jesus of Nazareth.

Psalm 2:7. Verse 7 is apparently a direct part of the ritual. In 2 Kings 11:12, we read that after the priest has anointed the king, he placed the crown on his head and "presented him with a copy of the covenant." In Psalm 2:7, the reference to the "Lord's decree" is the same as the testimony in Second Kings. The decree or testimony is the confirmation of the covenant with David. The content of the decree is "You are my Son; / I today have given birth to you" (my translation). The idea is that with the coronation, the king has been adopted as the son of God. He has been especially charged with God's power and God's responsibility.

At the conclusion of the decree, all nations are solemnly warned to worship only Yahweh and to serve only Yahweh's earthly representative, the king.

A similarity exists between this language and the language in the reports of the baptism of Jesus (see Mark 1:11 and the parallels).

Psalm 18. Psalm 18 is a long royal song of thanksgiving to God for a victory in battle. It describes first in poetic metaphors (verses 4-5) and then in vivid reality (verses 37-45) the distress of the king. It also provides astonishing divine imagery to describe the coming of God in power to serve the king (verses 6-19). Several of these passages are worth a closer look.

Psalm 18:4-5. The psalmist describes the king's problems in the most appalling of ways. Death was literally imminent. Without God, the king was lost. A few more words about the three "deathly" terms in these verses might be appropriate. *Sheol* ("the grave,") is a common Old Testament designation of the place every person goes at death. No one is punished or rewarded here. Sheol is the great leveler. One goes to Sheol regardless of age or station in life. Sheol is a yawning maw that swallows all and is never satisfied.

"Death" was a personified god in the Canaanite religion. All persons went to Death eventually. No one escaped from him. He was an altogether fearsome creature. Given the obvious antiquity of Psalm 18, the mention of death here might be intended to carry something of the personal terror of the old Canaanite god.

The third deadly term, "snares of death" ("torrents of perdition" in the New Revised Standard Version) is most often used in the Old Testament as a general term for wickedness or uselessness. In this passage, it certainly comes close to a wicked one, or a wicked thing.

These three terrifying terms are used to indicate the king's hopeless position before his enemies. Doom is sure. Destruction is inevitable!

Psalm 18:7-15. But in the highest heavens, there resides the Lord, the magnificent one, who alone is capable of snatching victory from the very jaws of death. Accompanied by the pyrotechnics of a thunderstorm, God descends on cherubim and flies in for the rescue. The imagery here is all old and all metaphorical. We are not to try to draw a picture of God using these verses. We are to feel the power, sense the majesty, and praise the victorious entrance of the only God who saves like this. The psalmist has all of these feelings, as the verses following verse 16 indicate.

Psalm 18:49-50. Because of God's great deeds for the king, the king will praise God to all nations. God is the one who grants David and his descendants an eternal throne. (See 2 Samuel 7.)

Psalm 20. This psalm is clearly representative of a worship experience. It is addressed to the king who has gone to the temple to petition God for help in some upcoming military struggle.

Psalm 20:1-3. The request begins by urging God to remember God's own past protection ("God of Jacob"). Then it indicates the place of God's help is centered on Zion, no doubt the very site of this prayer. God is then reminded of the king's faithfulness in performing the sacrificial, priestly work that is his to do.

Psalm 20:4-5. God is urged now to grant the king success in all he does, so that all the king's subjects may shout for joy in celebration of the victory.

Then, between verses 5 and 6 some oracle is given. A word of assurance is provided by priest or prophet to convince the king that his prayer has been heard and answered.

Psalm 20:6-9. Now the king can go forth renewed with the strength only God can provide. The king vows not to boast about his great military hardware, but to boast about God, who alone gives victory.

Psalm 21. This psalm is very carefully composed to make a clear distinction between the real power of the king and the source of that power, God. A problem always arises concerning the power of any leader who sometimes tries to challenge the ultimate authority and power of God. This psalm addresses that problem directly.

Psalm 21:1. In Hebrew, the opening reads "Yahweh, in your strength, the king rejoices." The order of the words—Yahweh, the strength of Yahweh, and then the king—indicates the psalmist's true interest.

Psalm 21:13. The ending of the psalm is exactly as the beginning. "Be exalted in your strength, LORD [same words as verse 1]; / we will sing and praise your might." Note, we do not praise the king's power, but God's power. One wonders whether this psalm was composed for the benefit of a king who exalted himself too highly. It is a reminder we all need to hear, even if we are not kings.

Psalm 45. This psalm is the only example in all Israelite psalm poetry of a true hymn to the king. In every other case, the object of the hymns of Israel is God alone. Given the king's central role in Israelite history, politics, and even religion, this is a remarkable fact. And even here, we do not have a purely royal hymn. The description of the king's glory is rooted in the word of blessing, a blessing that comes only from God, who alone anoints the king.

Psalm 45:1. The psalmist is described as stirred and anxious to proclaim words to the king filled with blessing.

Psalm 45:2-9. As one might imagine in patriarchal Israel, very little is said about the bride, but great poems are offered to the royal groom. This poem is a mixture of praise for his beauty and praise for his morality.

Psalm 45:10-12. However little the poet has to say about the future queen, there is a word of experienced advice for her.

> *Listen, daughter; look at me and bend your ear:*
> > *forget your people and your father's house,*
> > *then the king will desire your beauty.*
> *For he is our lord, so pay homage to him.*
> *Then the Tyrians will appear with gifts,*
> > *the richest of nations will seek your favor.*
> > > *(my translation)*

What may lie behind this advice is the fear of another Jezebel. Jezebel was the Tyrian princess who, far from forgetting who she was or where she came from, became a rabid missionary for the religion of Baal. (See 1 Kings 18–19; 21; and 2 Kings 9–10). May such never happen again, prays our poet.

Psalm 45:16-17. The psalm ends with assurance that these events will not happen again. The king is given the word that his son will live and be renowned more than his fathers and that the king's name itself shall live forever in the immortal words of this very psalm!

Psalm 72. You may note that the heading of this psalm is "Of Solomon." No doubt this title was derived from the lines in the poem where the "kings of Sheba" will bring gifts to the king (verse 10) and the suggestion of the king's son in verse 1. The former immediately calls to mind the legendary visit of the queen of Sheba to Solomon, recorded in 1 Kings 10:1-10. The title does not imply that Solomon wrote this psalm. It could just as easily mean that it was dedicated to Solomon.

Psalm 72:1-4. The psalm announces its emphasis very clearly. A literal translation would be, "God, your justice to the king, give, and your righteousness to the king's son." The key terms will be *justice* and *righteousness* in this psalm, and God's gift of them to the king will be the reason for praise. Verse 2 then explains what the king is to do with these two wonderful divine gifts. "May he judge your people in righteousness, / [especially] your afflicted ones with justice." In this, the king is judged by God and by history as effective or ineffective. Then verse 4 makes the charge to the king very specific.

> *May he dispense justice to the afflicted of the people,*
> > *give deliverance to needy children,*
> > *and crush the oppressor!*   *(my translation)*

The oppressed of the land look to the king for help. The king must be just if the justice of the land is to prevail. (See Jeremiah 22 for an attack on the unjust Jehoiakim.)

Psalm 72:5-7. In extravagant terms, the psalmist prays for a long reign for the just king. As long as sun and moon endure, so may the king live. And further, the psalmist asks that "righteousness flourish" and "prosperity abound," even until the disappearance of the moon! This latter phrase sounds like talk of more than just one earthly king. Surely, the psalmist is leaning toward that messianic figure who will bring justice that will outlive even the moon. The New Jerusalem in the Book of Revelation has no sun or moon at the time of God's final reign. (See Revelation 21:23.)

Psalm 72:12-14. All nations will serve this king, not because of his power and might, but because of his concern for the afflicted and needy.

Psalm 72:16-17. The psalm ends with the request for an abundance of grain and a multitude of people (see NRSV, verse 16c) due to the righteousness and justice of the king. Verse 17 reiterates one of the most important lines of the entire Old Testament tradition. In Genesis 12:1-3, Abram is called from his homeland to go to a land he has never seen. There God will bless him and will make his name a blessing so that, "all peoples on earth will be blessed through you." This same promise is reiterated to Jacob at Genesis 28:14. So here in Psalm 72:17 the king is to play the role of the mediator of blessing to the whole world. Later, Isaiah 49:6 reemphasizes God's call to the servant of Israel to be a "light for the Gentiles." In a nutshell, this is the framework for the missionary task of Israel as it moves through various Old Testament texts.

Psalm 72:18-20. These verses are not part of the original Psalm 72. They mark the close of Book II of the Psalter. (See Psalm 41:13 for the close of Book 1.) Verse 20 apparently closed a group of Davidic poems now included at this point in the Book of Psalms.

Psalm 89:1-37. This psalm is a royal lament, attributed to the king on a dark day of penance after a lost battle.

The poem begins with a lengthy psalm of praise, a hymn to the creative, sustaining power of God. First, the poet reminds God of God's eternal covenant with the anointed king, David and his descendants (verses 3-4). The creative powers of God are praised using the ancient creation mythology of Babylonians.

A brief retelling of the Babylonian myth of creation may prove helpful. In the beginning, there were two divine creatures, Tiamat, goddess of the salt water, and her consort, Apsu, god of the fresh water. Tiamat was a great dragon. She soon gave birth to the other lesser gods of wind, fire, and rain. But these lesser gods, led by Marduk, soon rebelled against their parents, and after long and roaring combat, defeated them. Marduk killed Tiamat and cut her carcass lengthwise. From the top half he made the sky and from the bottom half the earth.

In the myth, the helpers of Tiamat are subterranean creatures. In Job 9:13, the "cohorts of Rahab" (Rahab here is the sea monster, not a person) sound very much like these creatures. Obviously, there are connections between Rahab and this ancient myth. The reference to the "crushed Rahab" in verse 10 is similar to Tiamat's carcass from which Marduk fashioned the skies and the earth.

Once again, as in Psalm 18, the poet uses ancient ideas to improve the power of the presentation. And the fact that verse 11 goes on to talk precisely about the heavens (skies in Hebrew) and the earth makes the Babylonian myth reference all the more certain.

Verses 26-27 refer again to the adoption of the king as God's son in the same way Psalm 2 suggests this idea.

Psalm 89:38-51. But now the lament of the king begins. God has rejected and despised the formerly beloved, anointed one. God has "renounced the covenant," that supposedly eternal covenant with David, and has "defiled his crown in the dust" (verse 39). Then the plaintive cry comes from the king, "How long, Lord?" In verse 48, the question is who can "escape the power of the grave [Sheol]?" This question, you remember, was answered dramatically in Psalm 18. Only God can deliver a person from the bonds of Sheol. Here the question hangs in the air. God can perhaps deliver the king's soul, but will God do so?

Verse 51 hints that not only has the king lost the battle, but he has run away as well. The enemy is described as laughing at the footsteps of the king. The psalm ends in complete despair. Will God act now? How can Israel's king gain back his honor and power? These difficult questions remain unanswered by this psalm.

Psalm 89:52. Once again, this verse is not a part of Psalm 89. It closes Book III of the Psalms just as 41:13 closes Book I and 72:18-19 closes Book II. For this reason, the verse sounds like a doxology.

Psalm 110. This psalm clearly belongs to the ancient ritual of anointing the king. The king's throne in the ancient Near East was looked upon as a symbol of the throne of the deity. Thus, when God speaks in Psalm 110:1 to the king, God speaks from the throne and offers the king a seat at God's right hand.

Psalm 110:4. Melchizedek, the mysterious priest-king of Salem in Genesis 14:18, represents to the psalmist the union of royal and priestly power. In David and Solomon, priestly power was joined to royal power. But the rise of the organized priesthood threatened the priestly authority of the king. In Psalm 110, the king is granted priestly authority "forever, in the order of Melchizedek." That is, as that ancient man of worth was both priest and king, so shall the present king be. In this respect, one might read Psalm 110 as an anti-priestly psalm.

Melchizedek is not mentioned again in the Bible until the New Testament Letter of Hebrews. There he plays a fascinating and confusing role. At Hebrews 5:5-6, both Psalm 2 and Psalm 110 are quoted as applying directly to Jesus Christ. Jesus now is said to be a priest "in the order of Melchizedek," not like any typical human priests. Melchizedek is consequently a better priest than any other Israelite one. Then in Hebrews 7:1-10, this argument is extended. Jesus is an eternal priest, like Melchizedek, who is "without father or mother" (none is mentioned in the Bible). Because Jesus is immortal he is our high priest forever. Temporary, human priests are no longer needed. The author of Hebrews uses this strange figure, Melchizedek, in this way.

DIMENSION THREE:
WHAT DOES THE BIBLE MEAN TO ME?

The Concept of the Messiah

My interest in this subject is based on a feeling that there is profound ignorance about the ways Jesus did not fulfill the Jewish expectations of the Messiah for Israel. As is suggested in the participant book, the Jews did not expect that the Messiah would suffer and die as a substitute for all persons.

A Christian reading of certain Old Testament texts developed that view for Jesus of Nazareth, but no Jewish writer ever made such a connection. This clearly indicates that Jesus' horrible death would have effectively eliminated him from the category of Messiah, as it was defined by Jews.

The reason this strikes me as so important is that the lingering anti-Semitism of many Christians rests at least in part on the belief that the Jews rejected Jesus. We can hardly learn to love those whom we so terribly misunderstand and misrepresent.

I hope that the group can discuss this issue with some care. You can help class members learn to see the facts of the case for messianic expectations before reaching dangerous conclusions about the relationships between Jews and Christians.

The Great "I am"

Because God cannot be contained by human language, language about God is metaphorical. When Jesus called God "Father" he was using language of the first century in Palestine that had special connotations for his hearers. We share some of these connotations and not others. To call God "Father" is to use a metaphor for God. That metaphor becomes more than a literary device for the believer, however. We internalize it and use it as our operative relationship with God. If your experience of earthly fathers has been negative, such a metaphor may not be the best for you. The word *parent* may be better. Or you may prefer *nurturer*. Perhaps neither is personal enough for you and you want to put God's nurturing role into another family image that carries all the warmth and power of God's love for you. No limits can be placed on our God who can be all things.

It is important to realize that naming God in no way changes God's form or person. God is God, unchanged by human language. But in finding our comfortable relationship with God, we discover God's ability and willingness to be whatever person we need God to be.

God is ever-new. One of my favorite Bible passages is Isaiah 43:19. "See, I am doing a new thing! / Now it springs up; do you not perceive it?" We cannot allow ourselves to become fixed into one view of God, or one perception. If we believe God can and is doing a new thing, we must have our ears and eyes and other senses attuned to the new thing of God. After all, the God who came as a baby and who died on a cross is liable to do just about anything!

Images of how God comes to us must never become stale. If they do, we run the risk of not experiencing God's newness and of excluding those who have had a new experience. Encourage class members to be open to one another as they share their different perspectives of God's presence. Ask class members to seriously and thoughtfully consider each other's witness.

Close the session with a prayer for unity in diversity.

Shout for joy to God, all the earth! / Sing the glory of his name; / make his praise glorious! (66:1-2).

COMMUNAL THANKSGIVING PSALMS

DIMENSION ONE: WHAT DOES THE BIBLE SAY?

Answer these questions by reading Psalm 65

1. Where is God to be praised? (65:1, 4)

God is to be praised in Zion, that is, in the holy temple.

2. Why is praise due to God? (65:2, 5-8)

Praise is due to God because God answers prayer and does awesome and righteous deeds.

3. What do the streams of God provide? (65:9)

The streams of God provide water and grain for the people.

Answer these questions by reading Psalm 66

4. Who should shout for joy to God? (66:1)

All the earth should shout for joy to God.

5. What has God done that is worthy of praise? (66:5-7)

God turned the sea into dry land and keeps watch on the nations.

6. What does the worshiper do in response to God? (66:13-15)

The worshiper offers God burnt offerings in the temple.

Answer these questions by reading Psalm 67

7. Why will God be gracious to those who pray? (67:2)

God will be gracious so that God's ways may be known among all nations.

8. How does God deal with the world? (67:4)

God rules the people with equity and guides the nations.

9. How can we know that God is with us? (67:6)

When the land yields its harvest, we say that God has blessed us.

Answer these questions by reading Psalm 75

10. What do the worshipers say at the beginning of the psalm? (75:1)

The worshipers give thanks to God.

11. In whom is God most interested? (75:4)

God seems most concerned with the boastful and wicked.

Answer these questions by reading Psalm 100

12. How should God be worshiped? (100:2)

God should be worshiped with gladness.

13. Why should we praise the Lord as our God? (100:3)

We should praise the Lord because God has made us and we are God's people.

14. Why is the Lord good? (100:5)

God is good because God's faithfulness and love endure forever.

Answer these questions by reading Psalm 105

15. What is the key word in this psalm? (105:7-11)

    The key word is covenant.

16. What story is told in this psalm? (105:12-41)

    It is the story of Israel from the time of Abraham to the wandering in the desert.

17. What should be the people's response to God's great deeds? (105:45)

    The people should keep God's precepts and observe God's laws.

Answer these questions by reading Psalm 106

18. How is this story of God's great deeds different from that of Psalm 105? (106:6-7)

    This psalm emphasizes the sin of Israel's ancestors.

19. How does God respond to the continual sin of Israel? (106:44-46)

    God always relents because of the abundance of God's great love.

20. What should we do when we are saved by God? (106:47)

    We should give thanks to God's holy name.

Answer these questions by reading Psalm 136

21. What is the refrain of the psalm? (136:1, 2, and so on.)

    "His love endures forever."

22. Which deeds of God are emphasized here? (136:10-15)

    The events surrounding the Exodus are emphasized.

23. In whom is God finally interested? (136:25)

    God gives food to every creature; God is interested in all.

DIMENSION TWO:
WHAT DOES THE BIBLE MEAN?

The psalms covered in this lesson are Psalms 65, 66, 67, 75, 100, 105, 106, and 136. Psalms 107 and 124 are of the same type, but are not considered in this session.

I have emphasized the formal literary shape of this group of psalms to remind us that patterns of literature are important to the psalmists. Certain shapes were required at certain times. However, within the shape, the psalmist felt free to highlight various facets of the poem to match the specific needs of the worshiping congregation. The psalms might be compared to sonnets. The form of a sonnet is even more rigid than the communal thanksgiving form. Each sonnet has precisely fourteen lines, and the final couplet is always rhymed. Yet, within this form can be found a rich profusion of insight and language.

Psalm 65. The psalmists believed that when God is praised for past great deeds, those past deeds are again made present by the recitation of the psalm itself.

Psalm 65 is a psalm of thanksgiving that is intimately connected with the Israelite feast of harvest. The psalmist celebrates God's long-ago victory over the watery chaos in creation. At the same time, that earlier victory is used to indicate that God again has conquered the forces of darkness and has reestablished the right order of the world, now symbolized by the gift of rain. Verses 6-8 make this symbolism clear. This is the God

Who establishes the mountains with his strength,

being empowered with might;

who stills the roaring seas,

their roaring waves,

and the tumult of the peoples.

Those who dwell at the far reaches are awestruck by his signs.

The movements of morning and evening,

you caused to shout for joy. (my translation)

God's creation of the world is truly an awesome deed, but it is no one-time affair. God continues to do such deeds. Without God's gift of rain, described in 65:9-10, the forces of disorder would again prevail. The God who created the universe is the God who provides the rain.

To pray this psalm is to ask God to do again what God has done first in creation. We pray that God will make continual life possible in an ordered world.

Point out to the group how important speaking the psalm was for the Israelites. The psalm celebrates a God who is past, present, and future.

Psalm 66. The setting for this communal thanksgiving psalm is quite different from the harvest festival. Some terrible thing has happened to the community and is described as a time of God's testing (verse 10). Now the community has come to fulfill the vow to God made during the trouble.

Psalm 66:1-4. The whole earth is called to give thanks for God's awesome deeds. God's enemies (equivalent, no doubt, to the psalmist's enemies) have again been defeated.

Psalm 66:5-7. God's first awesome deed was turning the sea to dry land. We should not forget that the first time God did that was at the creation of the world, when God divided the sea to make dry land appear. (See Genesis 1:9-10.) Of course, the next line reminds us inevitably of the Red Sea event. Nor should we forget the miracle of the Jordan in Joshua 3. These initial victories of God over the raging waters are simply an indication of God's constant will to defeat raging forces that would thwart God's will. The "rebellious" of verse 7 are probably those who have been God's and the psalmist's enemies.

Psalm 66:10-12. The trouble that remains vague in the psalm was sent by God as a test, an examination. As silver is refined, so did God refine the Israelites to test their purity. Whatever the trouble was, God has provided victory.

Psalm 66:13-15. The psalmist has vowed to give proper worship and will now go to the temple and give it. For this psalmist proper worship was the burnt offering of appropriate animals. Such talk is naturally repugnant to modern ears and seems little more than barbaric primitivism. However, before we make simple value judgments, we need to ask why the Israelites made these sacrifices. No single answer can be given, but we can say that sacrifice was seen as the appropriate response to God's initial gifts of creation and life. When this psalmist vows to sacrifice to God and goes to do so, we may be certain that he is not simply paying a debt, nor feeding God (as some earlier primitives thought), nor keeping away God's anger. The sacrifice of animals was made as the valuable and serious gift to God who had demonstrated love for the people in grace.

Psalm 66:16. The psalmist publicly proclaims God's great deeds on the people's behalf.

Psalm 67. Like Psalm 65, this psalm must have had a close connection to the harvest festival. And, as in the earlier psalm, God's ruling leads directly to the bounty of the earth. The very structure of the poem shows the cycle of blessing and bounty offered by the just God.

Psalm 67:1. "May God be gracious to us and bless us" pleads the first line.

Psalm 67:2. Then, when God's grace is truly received and acknowledged, God's way will be known on earth and God's salvation among all nations.

Psalm 67:4. God's grace is evidenced in God's equity and in God's guidance of all the nations.

Psalm 67:6-7. God's blessing is now evident in the harvest. "The land yields its harvest; / God, our God, blesses us." Thus, the psalm begins with a petition to God for blessing and grace. Note also that the psalm ends with blessing and abundance. The reality of God's grace preceding God's blessing is made clear in the very shape of Psalm 67, where grace precedes blessing.

After reading Psalm 67, one might be tempted to say, "I am rich; God has blessed me. After all, does not this psalm say that abundance is the very proof of God's blessing?" What makes this view dangerous and ultimately wrong is that in verse 4 God judges all nations equally and comforts all nations on earth. On an earth where God's equality is not matched by human concern with equality, no person can boast of God's exclusive blessing while others starve. And persons cannot utter that blasphemy that "they starve because God has not blessed them." God wills blessing and grace for all, as this group of psalms made especially clear.

Psalm 75. This psalm partakes of the same tradition as Psalms 46, 48, and 76 (see Lesson 3). These psalms deal with the historic and ever-repeated victory of God over all foes. As in those psalms, we ought not to look for any one historical victory. The song merely celebrates in very dramatic language the assurance of God's final victory over all wicked persons.

Psalm 75:4. The symbol of the horn is used in two interesting ways in this psalm and serves to unite the poem. In verse 4, *horn* is power. The command from the oracle to the wicked, "do not lift your horns," will be matched at the end of the psalm by God's lifting up of the horns of the righteous.

Psalm 75:6-7. No "exalting" (again the same verb as "lifting up") comes from any human source, not from any settled areas either east or west or from the desert. Only God "exalts" and "brings down."

Psalm 75:8. The image of the cup of poisonous wrath has an interesting history. It may have originated with Jeremiah who used it first to describe God's displeasure with Israel (see Jeremiah 8:14; 9:15). Later in Jeremiah, the cup of wrath is extended to all nations (see Jeremiah 25:15; 49:12). The unknown prophet of the Exile, whom we call the Second Isaiah, takes the image and reverses its meaning. God now removes the poisonous cup from the people Israel who have drunk their fill and have been exiled (see Isaiah 51:22). The symbol returns in a most dramatic way in Revelation. The cup of wrath is drunk by the beast (John's image of profound evil), the scarlet woman (the symbol of Babylon/Rome), and Babylon itself twice (see Revelation 14:10; 16:19; 17:4; 18:6). Thus, this symbol of the cup of God's wrath extends over 700 years through the biblical tradition. In Psalm 75:8, the cup is given to the wicked who will ultimately drink it down to the dregs.

Psalm 75:10. The earlier image of the wicked lifting up their horns is now contrasted by God's cutting off the horns of the wicked. (The Hebrew text reads "I will cut off," but the king could be speaking now on behalf of God's actions.) God's action of cutting off the horns reminds us of some other Old Testament occasions when the horns of the altar were cut off.

The altar of the ancient temple had four protuberances, one at each corner, called horns. (See, for example, Leviticus 4:7, 18, 25.) On several occasions in the life of Israel the horns of the altar, the final place of safety, proved ineffective. Two instances come readily to mind. When Solomon became king, after the death of David, Adonijah, his older half-brother, gave up his attempt at the throne. In fear of his life, he ran to the house of worship and grabbed the horns of the altar, claiming sanctuary. He was spared that time, but killed soon after. David's faithful general, Joab, was not so lucky. He grabbed those same horns claiming safety, but was hacked to death on the very spot. Amos, in the same grisly metaphor, claims that there will be no escape from God's wrath for the faithless Israel. "The horns of the altar will be cut off" (Amos 3:14).

With the background of the cup and horn images, one can appreciate the literary skill of this psalmist all the more.

Psalm 100. All lands are called to praise the God who made us to be God's people. The worshipers are called to the house of worship (verse 4) where God's goodness, unfailing love, and faithfulness are affirmed as God's blessings. A few words about these key terms used to describe God may be appropriate.

God is good. An extremely general term in Hebrew, it means quite simply good in every variety of the meaning. It includes pleasant, useful, efficient, beautiful, kind, right, and morally good. To say that God is good is at the same time to say very little and a great deal if the broad meaning of the term is kept in the background.

God's love endures forever. I have discussed this term in Lesson 1 in connection with Psalm 33:5. Here it must be emphasized that solidarity between partners is the essence of love (*hesed* in Hebrew). See the fuller discussion in Lesson 1 (page 22).

God's faithfulness continues through all generations. The basic meaning of this term is steadiness or immobility. Reliability is also part of this term. God's word and actions are all of these things generation after generation. Our common word, *amen*, comes from this word. When we say *amen*, we affirm that whatever we have just said is steady, reliable, certain.

Psalm 105. The emphasis in this psalm lies in its covenant interest (verses 7-11) and in its historical retelling of God's great deeds from Abraham to the gift of the Promised Land.

Psalm 105:7-11. Here the original patriarchal covenant that was made with Abraham, sworn to Isaac, and established for Jacob as a statute, is defined exclusively as a promise for the land of Canaan. The ensuing hymnic tale of how Israel saw the covenant fulfilled is based on the definition of the covenant, specifically as a covenant of land.

The subject of covenant in the Bible is extremely important and complex. A covenant is a solemn promise made binding by oath and is often accompanied by religious sanctions of some kind. The covenant may be struck verbally or through symbolic actions. In either case, the parties to the covenant recognize the actions as binding on them to fulfill the promises made. Covenants in the Old Testament include the covenants with Noah (Genesis 9), Abraham (Genesis 15; 17), and the Sinai covenant with Israel (Exodus 19–20). In Psalm 105, the covenant with Abraham is the one written about.

Psalm 105:12-41. Several interesting verses appear in this litany of Israel's past and God's dealing with that past. Verses 14-15 are apparent references to Genesis 12:17 and 20:3 where kings were rebuked. Abraham, in each case, came out of the confrontation a rich man. In verse 15, one finds the only time in the Old Testament that "anointed ones" (*messiah*) is applied to the patriarchs. Here it is a synonym for prophets, a role played by Abraham in Genesis 20:7.

In verses 16-22, the story of Joseph is told, emphasizing the fulfillment of the dreams given to Joseph by God. The dramatized account in verse 18 of Joseph's great pain in slavery is completely absent from the Genesis account. Verses 23-38 recount the events leading to the Exodus, reiterating always that God was the chief actor in the drama. Note that verse 25 may be an oblique reference to God's famous hardening of Pharaoh's heart. No mention of the events at the Red Sea is made. Verses 39-41 briefly recount God's miraculous provision of food and water in the desert. All these events occurred because God "remembered his holy promise [the covenant] / given to his servant Abraham" (verse 42).

Psalm 105:43-45. God's part of the covenant is now fulfilled. God has provided them the "lands of the nations." They now possess "what others had toiled for." This idea recalls Deuteronomy's insistence that Israel did not do anything, either to get the land, or to make it fruitful. God did it all (see Deuteronomy 6:10-12). Now Israel must keep its share of the covenant by keeping God's statutes and observing God's laws. The word *laws* is *Torah* in Hebrew. Its more accurate translation should be teaching. God's will for humanity, what God wants all humanity to know and to do, is God's *Torah*.

Psalm 106. Psalm 105 was a straightforward prayer of thanksgiving to God. Psalm 106 is, on the contrary, a confessional thanksgiving to God to forgive the nearly continuous sin of the chosen people.

Psalm 106:6-43. This time the story picks up in Egypt. Verse 6 indicates the solidarity of sin between the contemporary psalmist and his ancestors. Verse 7 probably refers to Exodus 14:10-12 when the Israelites panic at the sight of Pharaoh bearing down on them with his chariots. Nevertheless, God saved the ungrateful ones. After the great victory, the psalmist adds sarcastically in verse 12 that "then they believed his promises." But verse 13 pictures again the unfaithful people. Now in the desert the people cry for food. Again God provides, but sends a plague ("wasting disease") as well for their unfaithfulness. (See Numbers 11:4-6, 31-35.) Another sign of the people's apostasy, the rebellion against Moses (see Numbers 16), is recounted in verses 16-18.

The psalmist then recounts the famous sin of the golden calf (Exodus 32) and reminds the readers that without the intercession of Moses all of them would have been destroyed by God's anger. Then as the people finally approached the Promised Land, they refused to enter it out of fear (Numbers 14:1-35). God condemned all of them to fall in the desert without setting foot in the land at all. Verses 28-31 recount the apostasy to the god Baal of Peor (Numbers 25:1-13). Phinehas, in a violent act, averts the plague of God, not unlike Moses' intercession in Exodus 32. Verses 32-33 tell of the testing of God at the waters of Meribah (Numbers 20:2-13; compare Exodus 17:1-7).

The tale of sin goes on into the time of the judges, even after the entry into the land (verses 34-39). (See Judges 2:11-19.) Verses 40-43 affirm that Israel has not changed in history from the time of Egypt. Fortunately, neither has God, who always hears their cry. God's great love has always kept the people no matter where their evil has caused them to be (verse 46).

This psalm affirms a significant idea about the grace of God found in both the Old and the New Testaments. Deuteronomy 7:7-8 reminds the Israelites that God's love has nothing to do with righteousness or lack of it. God loves the people and has chosen them. They did not earn God's love. But this is surely like Paul's New Testament claim that Christ died for us while we were sinners, which is proof that God loves us. (See Romans 5:8.) Our sin does not exclude God's love; it provides renewed occasion for it. Here, one might say, the unity of the two testaments is manifest in the love of God offered for the sinner.

Psalm 136. This psalm begins with God's creation of the world (verses 5-9). Verses 7-9 clearly refer to Genesis 1. Verses 10-15 give the story of the Exodus with special attention to the miracle at the Red Sea. The desert (verse 16) was remembered often as a time of incredible apostasy by Israel. The gift of the land is then recounted as God's great gift. The defeat of the two kings, Sihon and Og, is tied up with the gift of the land (see Numbers 21:21-35).

At the end of this lengthy poem of God's revelation in Israelite history, verse 25 emphasizes the universality of God's gift of food. The God revealed in Israel's history is none other than the "God of heaven" (verse 26) who gives food to all.

DIMENSION THREE:
WHAT DOES THE BIBLE MEAN TO ME?

God's Work in History

I have chosen only one issue to address in connection with these communal thanksgiving psalms. It is an important issue for us to think about in a community of faith.

History is never just the cold record of facts in any book. By the very fact of writing history, the historian interprets what he or she is writing. In *Genesis* (Westminster Press, 1971), Gerhard von Rad has described biblical history as "a view and interpretation not only of that which once was but of a past event that is secretly present and decisive for the present."

What counts is not the details or the proof of a past event but how that event is "decisive for the present." Von Rad goes on to describe the real function of the psalms we have looked at in this lesson (even though he is himself referring to the stories of Genesis and Exodus).

> It is the saga [his word for those stories, but it is applicable to the psalmist's use of the stories], much more than historical writing, that knows this secret contemporary character of apparently past events; it can let things become contemporary in such a way that everyone detects their importance, while the same events would probably have been overlooked by historical writing. . . . For there is another history that a people makes besides the externals of wars, victories, migrations, and political catastrophes. It is an inner history, one that takes place on a different level, a story of inner events, experiences, and singular guidance, of working and becoming mature in life's mysteries. . . .[1]

Christians should know this fact more than most people. For about two thousand years now Christians have rallied around an event "overlooked by historical writing." Outside the Gospels there is not a single clear contemporary reference to any event of the life you and I hold as central to our existence. Jesus was simply overlooked by history. But his life and death and resurrection have led us to become more mature in life's mysteries. We know that Napoleon lost the battle of Waterloo in 1815, but that fact is not decisive for us today. The life of Jesus—avoided, overlooked by history—is. And for the psalmists, Israel's past only has meaning when it can be appropriated and celebrated by their contemporary worshipers.

Ask class members to share their answers to the questions posed in the participant book. Close the discussion by reciting Psalm 136 as it was probably originally done. Read the first verse and have the group respond with the refrain.

[1] Gerhard von Rad, *Genesis* (Westminster Press, 1971); page 33.

When I felt secure, I said, / "I will never be shaken" (30:6).

INDIVIDUAL THANKSGIVING PSALMS

DIMENSION ONE: WHAT DOES THE BIBLE SAY?

Answer these questions by reading Psalm 30

1. Why does the psalmist exalt the Lord? (30:1-2)

    God has healed the psalmist.

2. Who is to sing praises to the Lord? (30:4)

    God's faithful people are to sing praises to the Lord.

3. How long does God's anger last? (30:5)

    God's anger lasts only a moment.

Answer these questions by reading Psalm 32

4. What happened when the psalmist kept silent? (32:3)

    The bones of the psalmist wasted away.

5. Who should offer prayer to God? (32:6)

    All the faithful should offer prayer to God.

6. Why shouldn't we be like the horse or the mule? (32:8-9)

We must have understanding, not having to "be controlled by bit and bridle."

Answer these questions by reading Psalm 34

7. When will the psalmist extol the Lord? (34:1)

The psalmist will extol the Lord at all times.

8. Whom does God especially see and hear? (34:15)

God especially sees the righteous and hears their cry.

9. The Lord is close to whom? (34:18)

The Lord is close to the brokenhearted.

Answer these questions by reading Psalm 40

10. How many wonders has God done for us? (40:5)

God has done so many wonders that they would be "too many to declare."

11. What does God not desire? (40:6)

God does not desire sacrifice and offering.

12. What is in the heart of the psalmist? (40:8)

God's law is in the heart of the psalmist.

Answer these questions by reading Psalm 41

13. What seems to be the problem of this psalmist? (41:3)

The psalmist seems to have had some terrible disease.

14. Who has turned against the psalmist? (41:5, 9)

Enemies and the psalmist's "close friend" have turned against the psalmist.

15. How does the psalmist know that God is there? (41:11)

The psalmist has not been beaten by an enemy.

Answer these questions by reading Psalm 92

16. When should God be praised? (92:2)

God should be praised both morning and night.

17. What are the wicked compared to? (92:7)

The wicked are like grass.

18. What are the righteous compared to? (92:12)

The righteous are like a palm tree and a cedar.

Answer these questions by reading Psalm 116

19. Why does the psalmist love the Lord? (116:1)

The psalmist loves the Lord because the Lord has heard his voice and cry for mercy.

20. Who causes "alarm" in the psalmist? (116:11)

All those who are liars cause his alarm.

21. What does the psalmist offer to God? (116:17)

The psalmist sacrifices a thank offering.

Answer these questions by reading Psalm 118

22. Who should proclaim "his love endures forever"? (118:1-4)

Israel, the house of Aaron, and those who fear the Lord should proclaim it.

23. For what is the psalmist thankful to God? (118:10)

The psalmist defeated his enemies in the name of the Lord.

24. What should we do in the day that God has made? (118:24)

We should rejoice and be glad.

DIMENSION TWO:
WHAT DOES THE BIBLE MEAN?

This lesson is the second lesson on songs of thanksgiving. The psalms covered in this lesson are Psalms 30, 32, 34, 40, 41, 92, 116, and 118. Psalms 103, 111, and 138 are of the same type, but are not considered in this session.

What differentiates these psalms from the songs of lament, which we will examine in Lessons 7 through 11, is one very simple fact. In the psalms of thanksgiving, God is praised in response to some act of help, healing, or salvation that the psalmist has felt to have come from God. In the psalms of lament, the psalmist calls to God in anticipation of some divine act.

In the psalms for this lesson, the emphasis is to be found on the saving deed of God. Even in the midst of the most disturbing and troubling times, God is praised and affirmed as deliverer and helper. When the Jews entered the gas chambers of Auschwitz and Dachau, many reports suggested that they were singing psalms. These psalms were often their last words. Such power! That power that comes from faith in God's availability to us needs to be ours as we study these psalms.

Psalm 30. This psalm gives us an insight into the continuing and historic use and reuse of the psalms. The Israelites tended to use their familiar songs rather than new ones at occasions that called for great celebration or great mourning. They returned to these again and again. They are familiar and memorable. But more than that, each repeated use gives them an extra layer of veneration. To know that Psalm 23 has been used in funeral services for centuries is a great source of power that far transcends the familiarity of the words.

Psalm 30 was connected with the temple dedication, as the title suggests. That this dedication was in fact a rededication of the temple seems clear from the psalm's content. The psalmist records God's momentary anger, but also God's refusal to let the "enemies gloat over" him. This was composed to be an individual poem. However, when the Maccabeans defeated the Syrian Greeks they cleansed the temple of Jerusalem, earlier profaned by Antiochus, to the accompaniment of Psalm 30. (See First Maccabees in the Apocrypha.)

Psalm 30:2. The verb translated healed is usually used in contexts of health and disease, sometimes with the extended meaning of fixing something broken, such as a relationship. The use of the word demonstrates the original health concern of the author. God has healed disease and is therefore worthy of praise.

Psalm 30:6-7. In these verses, the psalmist admits to overconfidence that led to a disastrous fall from ease. The psalmist was hardly prepared for this fall.

Psalm 30:8-9. God's hidden face forced the psalmist to cry out bitterly, "What is gained if I am silenced?" The more startling theological cry is "Will the dust praise you?" The answer to this sharp rhetorical question is, of course, "no." Those who have died and turned to dust do not praise God. This strain is familiar in the psalms and is found in Psalms 115:17, 6:5, and 88:12. The meaningless, shadowy realm of Sheol contains no praise of God.

But, as often in the psalms, one can find some words on the other side of the issue. Psalm 139 holds that God leads and guides even in Sheol. If God can be present even there, perhaps praise of God may appear anywhere.

Psalm 32:1. The psalmist begins with the praise of the God who forgives transgression and sin. Later the psalmist admits to being unwilling at first to admit any sin (verse 3). As a result the psalmist's body was racked with disease.

The word translated blessed also has the secular meaning of happy. In the mind of the psalmists, those who are happy are at the same time those who are blessed. But, as we admit this, we should be very careful not to take an oversimplified view of what is suggested by the equation of happy and blessed. If you are feeling well, you assume that your blessings are great. If you are doing poorly, you assume that your blessings are few. But from that rather human analysis, it is a long and dangerous leap to the general belief that happy persons are blessed by God, while unhappy ones are cursed by God. The Bible contains traditions that suggest that view, but other traditions in the Bible, notably Job, reject such a view completely.

Psalm 32:8-9. These verses show us that the wisdom tradition has a great concern for teaching, for probing difficult subjects and ideas, and for extending the boundaries of thought about both sacred and secular matters. God is described as a teacher here. But the psalmist is really the one who is so characterized. Yet, God provides the inspiration for the psalmist's claim to be a teacher of others.

Psalm 32:10. This verse is a typical teaching of the wisdom school.

Psalm 34. The connection of this psalm with David's false insanity before Abimelek (actually Achish) is an interesting, if unexplainable, historical use of the psalm. The story of David's show of insanity is peculiar enough in itself. After he was taken to Achish, the king of Gath, he wildly wrote graffiti on the walls of the city while spittle ran down his beard. (See 1 Samuel 21:12-15.) The king demanded that he be removed. Achish told his own people that he had enough crazy folk without adding this foreign lunatic to the group. The story seems to suggest David's unwillingness to have a relationship with the Philistines, even though Saul was trying to kill him.

This psalm's relationship to the Samuel story is strange. The incident of David's false madness seems hardly worth remembering, let alone worthy of a whole psalm. But David was the great king, and as Israel's history progressed the memory of him grew. Eventually all talk of a renewed Israel always included a king like David. For this reason, when Jesus rode into Jerusalem on a donkey the crowds shouted, "Hosanna to the Son of David."

Psalm 34:2, 6. Two familiar words are used to describe the righteous one in the psalm to whom God especially gives attention. Verse 2 speaks of the "afflicted" who are to hear and rejoice. This word is most often used in the Old Testament in the context of oppression, sometimes violent oppression of one group or person by another group or person. The prophets use the term to attack the wealthy who oppress the poor. In the psalm, the word is used in a general sense to describe the psalmist as an afflicted one who is judged righteous by God. The same could be said of the word *poor* in verse 6. Its specific concern of economic and social justice has disappeared in this psalm.

One can see a dangerous movement taking place. The specific concerns of the poor and the afflicted, articulated so glaringly by the prophets, have become here general statements that are hard to grasp. When we generalize the terms *righteous* or *poor*, we lose our specific concern for individuals who are poor or afflicted. To create faceless groups of human beings is to forget that human beings are individually unique.

Psalm 34:8. This has always been an interesting and unusual use of the word *taste*. Two other similar usages might shed light on its use here. In Proverbs 31:18, the word *sees* is literally *tastes*. An even more interesting use is found in the story of David's false madness in 1 Samuel 21:12-15. The New Revised Standard Version translates verse 13 "so he changed his *behavior* before them" (italics added). Could the use of this rather unusual term be one reason the psalm was connected to this David story?

Psalm 40:6-8. The very heart of the psalm is found in these verses. Here is my translation.

> *Sacrifice and offering you do not want;*
> > *rather you have dug ears for me.*
> > *Burnt offering and sin offering you have not requested.*
> *Then I said, "Look! I am coming!*
> > *In the scroll of the book it is written about me."*
> *To do your will, My God, I wait;*
> > *Your Torah is in my belly.*

God does not want sacrifice and offering (verse 6). This psalmist is saying that nothing he does could ever satisfy God's will. By offering sacrifices the Israelites might come to think they are gaining favor from God. On the contrary, this psalmist is completely at the disposal of God. The odd expression "you have dug ears for me" means God has acted on the psalmist to make him ready to act on God's behalf.

Psalm 40:7. The psalmist is ready to be God's servant. The "scroll" is an interesting concept. The idea of a divine scroll containing God's will appears in the Bible at some significant places. Jeremiah 15:16 says that the prophet ate words that he had found, and they were joy for him, but they isolated him from his fellow Israelites. Ezekiel 3:1-3 speaks of this prophet eating a scroll that was sweet to him. The image is extended in Zechariah 5:1-4 into a "flying scroll" that is a curse to the whole land. And finally, in Revelation, John is called to eat a scroll that is both bitter and sweet (Revelation 10:8-11). Another facet of this idea is found in Daniel 7:10. The divine court meets in judgment and "the books were opened." Here we have books filled with deeds of persons who are judged by God. The scroll of God's book contains the psalmist's name, making the psalmist certain that God is calling.

Psalm 40:8. We must remember that the Hebrew word *Torah* means far more than "law." It means "teaching, instruction," in effect a whole way of life. The psalmist claims to have God's Torah in his heart (NRSV says *belly*). The heart is the place of intellect and will. The belly is the seat of the emotions and desires. The Hebrews had no word for *mind* or *brain*. The psalmist claims to have internalized God's Torah so that it has literally become a part of the psalmist's body.

These verses are quoted in the New Testament Letter to the Hebrews, 10:5-7. The author of Hebrews identifies the speaker of these verses as Christ and claims that Christ has done away with all sacrifice by sacrificing himself for all.

Psalm 41. The idea of this psalm is quite familiar. God is praised, the problem is described (illness), God saves, and the sufferer tells of being reunited with God. What makes this psalm different from an individual thanksgiving psalm is the glimpse it gives us of a magical world that most of us no longer share. The psalmist is convinced that his enemies and even his bosom friend are using magic words and acts to increase the sickness and the pain of the psalmist. One gets the clear implication of a great conspiracy of magic trained solely on the sufferer.

Other biblical passages show us something of this magic world. Proverbs 6:12-15 gives us the picture of a wicked man, going through some rites of evil designed to "stir up conflict." Psalm 27:12 pictures adversaries who speak evil by "spouting malicious accusations" or dark incantations for evil purposes. Three prophetic texts hint at this world, too. Isaiah 32:7 and 58:9 talk of evil signs and acts, while Ezekiel 13:18 speaks directly of witchlike women leading persons astray. In our own day, some persons believe in the occult and in the power of magic. In Israel, a far less scientific world than our own, any number of persons retained beliefs in the mysterious power of magic. This psalm affirms that God can overcome even those awesome powers.

Psalm 92:2. The use of the familiar terms, *love* (*hesed*) and *faithfulness*, recalls again Exodus 34:6. There God is revealed in a way that profoundly affected much later Israelite theological thought. This theological belief lies at the very center of the psalms of thanksgiving. The psalmist first proclaims that God is like that and then bases the cry of help on that belief.

Psalm 92:6-14. This psalm contains some of the favorite imagery of the wisdom traditions of Israel.

Psalm 92:6. The words "senseless people" are used in the first part of verse 6. The Hebrew word has an animal ring to it in the sense of being brutish. This animal image is contrasted with that of verse 10 where the horn (power) of the righteous one is exalted (or strengthened) like that of wild oxen. In the second line of verse 6, the word "fools" has a sense of insolence and dullness mixed. The expression "any fool can see" captures something of the sarcasm of verse 6.

Psalm 92:7. The second type of wisdom imagery is that of the plant world. The perfect vegetable image for the wicked is grass—they come up in bunches but die quickly at the slightest problem.

Psalm 92:12. On the contrary, the righteous are palm trees and cedars, long-lived plants of great height, power, usefulness, and fruitfulness.

Such animal and vegetable imagery is an excellent teaching device and memory aid. However, it also tends to simplify problems that are far more complex in reality. Calling persons brutes who question the inevitable demise of all wicked persons does not encourage serious discussion of the question. These psalms are not arguing theology though. They are proclaiming and celebrating the power of God as the psalmists saw it.

Psalm 116. In this straightforward individual psalm of thanksgiving, the psalmist vows to praise God and to offer God sacrifice because God has heard the cry for help. Death was imminent, as verses 3 and 8 make clear. But God, who alone controls life and death, brought the psalmist out of danger.

Psalm 116:10-11. I would translate verses 10-11 as follows:

I stood firm when I said,
  "I am greatly afflicted."
I said in my terrified haste,
  "All humans are idol worshipers."

The psalmist did not turn to easy human answers in desperation, but maintained a relationship to God and waited only for God's help. Crying out in pain is not a bad thing. One does not thereby deny faith. Faithful people are not always happy. Pain is a part of life and thus a part of faith.

Psalm 116:12-14, 17-18. This psalmist responds to God with traditional vows and sacrifice, both public and private. The author of Psalm 40 had a different response, as we noted.

Psalm 118:2-4. Three groups are called to say the refrain. "Israel" apparently refers to the chosen people of God. "House of Aaron" refers to the priestly officials of the temple. "Those who fear the LORD" may be any other persons, non-Israelite and non-priest, who worship God. This attempt to be inclusive emphasizes the relationship of this psalm to the worshiping community.

Psalm 118:22-23. You can probably begin to see just how the authors of the New Testament combed the Old Testament for examples and ideas to explain the life, death, and resurrection of Jesus. Some of your group may find these to be prophecies, predicting the coming of Jesus. Others may think of them as material found suitable for description after the fact. Whichever way these passages are viewed, they are examples of how the biblical tradition is a living tradition. Passages are not forever locked into their original contexts, but are found ever-new.

DIMENSION THREE: WHAT DOES THE BIBLE MEAN TO ME?

Psalm 32:3—Is There Punishment for Sin?

The struggle with this question has gone on since the beginning of recorded history. Some of our oldest documents refer to the problems of evil and good, and how they relate to divine reality. You and I are not going to solve this problem in one lesson from the Psalms. The Bible does not have one simple teaching to offer.

Within two broad biblical answers you might find some help. Genesis 3 tells us that human will brings forth the disharmony of a creation made by God for harmony. God is not implicated at all in the evil of the world. However, Isaiah 45:7 says clearly that God does all things. Can both be true? Is it possible to have a world of absolute human freedom and absolute divine control? And does God run a world where sin is always punished and righteousness always rewarded? The Bible again sets the limits for our discussion, but does not provide an easy answer. Use these two biblical references to address this problem in your group.

No Immortality in the Psalms

Does it surprise you to find that no talk of eternal life or immortality is contained in the psalms? I am always surprised when I think about the great depth of ethical reflection in the Old

Testament without any suggestions that all wrongs are righted, all hurts redressed, in some sort of afterlife. I attribute this fact to the deep feeling on the part of the Israelites that God was a God of life, a God who willed wholeness and beauty for the people. But they also believed God had provided well-defined ways to attain such wholeness and beauty. The Israelites felt no threat of eternal punishment or damnation was needed to coerce persons into good behavior. As Exodus 19:6 says, God has called Israel to be a "kingdom of priests and a holy nation." As God was holy, so the people, too, must be holy. When God claims a nation or a people, holy behavior is produced without fear or expectation of the result. God wills wholeness. If we love God as God loves us, we will strive for wholeness. No threat of eternal damnation will make us do otherwise.

People often ask me what I believe about immortality and eternal life. I know only one thing: God is wherever I am. In that sense, Psalm 139 is my psalm. Beyond that great claim, I know nothing about who, when, what, or why. Those questions I leave to God. I wonder whether we might learn from the Israelites' apparent lack of concern about this issue.

Ask the group to respond to the statement "No clear reference to eternal life is in the psalms." Are they sad, mad, or glad? Do they agree or disagree? How does the statement make any difference to them?

My God, my God, why have you forsaken me? (22:1).

7

INDIVIDUAL LAMENTS

DIMENSION ONE:
WHAT DOES THE BIBLE SAY?

Answer these questions by reading Psalm 3

1. What are the psalmist's foes saying? (3:2)

> *The psalmist's foes are saying, "God will not deliver him."*

2. What does the psalmist ask of God? (3:7)

> *The psalmist asks God to arise and deliver him.*

3. How does God respond? (3:7)

> *God strikes the enemies on the jaw and breaks the teeth of the wicked.*

Answer these questions by reading Psalm 5

4. When is the psalmist praying? (5:3)

> *The psalmist prays in the morning.*

5. Where does the psalmist want to go? (5:7)

> *The psalmist wants to enter God's house, the temple.*

6. How does the psalmist describe the enemies? (5:9)

> *The enemies have untrustworthy mouths, destructive hearts, gravelike throats, and deceitful tongues.*

Answer these questions by reading Psalm 6

7. What is the psalmist's condition? (6:2-3)

    The psalmist is in anguish; faint, with his bones in agony.

8. Can God be praised from the grave? (6:5)

    No one praises God from the grave (Sheol).

9. What will happen to the psalmist's enemies? (6:10)

    All the enemies will be ashamed, dismayed, and disgraced.

Answer these questions by reading Psalm 7

10. How does the psalmist proclaim innocence? (7:3-5)

    The psalmist swears that if there is any guilt in him that his enemies should overtake and trample him.

11. What does the psalmist want God to do? (7:6, 8)

    God must arise and judge the peoples.

12. What does the psalmist vow to do? (7:17)

    The psalmist vows to give thanks to God and sing praise to God.

Answer these questions by reading Psalm 9

13. What has happened to the enemy? (9:6)

    Endless ruins have overtaken the enemy; their cities and their memory destroyed.

14. Who seeks the Lord? (9:9-10)

    The oppressed and those who trust the Lord seek God.

15. If God answers, what will the psalmist do? (9:14)

    The psalmist will declare his praise and rejoice in God's salvation.

Answer these questions by reading Psalm 10

16. What are the first questions of the psalmist? (10:1)

    Why does God stand far off and hide?

17. What is the wicked person's chief statement? (10:4, 6)

    The wicked person has no room in his thoughts for God and thinks instead that he will never be shaken or harmed.

18. What will God finally do? (10:17-18)

    God will hear and strengthen the afflicted and defend the fatherless and the oppressed.

Answer these questions by reading Psalm 14

19. What does the fool say? (14:1)

    The fool says, "There is no God."

20. Are there any good people? (14:3)

    No one does good, not even one.

21. What will God do for Israel? (14:7)

    God will restore the fortunes of Israel.

Answer these questions by reading Psalm 22

22. Does God answer the psalmist? (22:2)

    God, at first, does not answer the psalmist.

23. How does the psalmist describe the problem? (22:12-18)

    The psalmist speaks of bulls, lions, bones out of joint, a melting heart, dryness in the throat, and a pack of ravenous dogs.

24. Who will finally worship God? (22:27)

    All the families of the nations will worship God.

DIMENSION TWO:
WHAT DOES THE BIBLE MEAN?

The psalms covered in this lesson are Psalms 3, 5, 6, 7, 9, 10, 14, and 22. Psalms 4, 13, 17, and 25 are of the same type, but are not examined in this lesson.

The laments of the Psalter are by far the largest group of psalms. They speak sharply and directly to God. They plead, urge, demand, and warn. Some of the language seems to us to border on the edge of blasphemy. How can one presume to talk to God like that? But the sharp tone and furious quality of some of these poems simply suggests a close relationship between God and worshiper and a great certainly that God really does care and does react to God's people.

Psalm 3:1. This lament psalm follows the pattern well. The request is the simple "LORD." The address has a desperate, heartfelt quality, however simple it may appear. No frills, no great adjectives are used here. God is simply addressed with urgency.

Psalm 3:1-2. Immediately, the complaint is lodged. The psalmist's foes are vast, and a large number of them are rising up against the psalmist. (The Hebrew word translated many would be better as vast.) And this same vast host is saying about the psalmist, "God will not deliver him." By speaking in this way, the psalmist establishes two facts. First, the enemies are out of control, a vast sea of antagonism and hatred. Second, they (the enemy) think that God will not help the psalmist. This latter statement is clearly an attempt to move God to do that very thing! The implication is that God had better help the psalmist to prove them wrong.

Psalm 3:3-4. Here is a more direct appeal to God, coupled with a statement of trust. God is described by the psalmist as a shield and as one who raises the psalmist's head. In contrast, the enemies rise against the psalmist (verse 1).

God is described as a shield sixteen times in the Old Testament. Of those sixteen, twelve are in the Book of Psalms. Many scholars believe that the Hebrew word for *shield* may have been an ancient name for God. The verb from which the noun *shield* comes means to "deliver" or "save."

The psalmist cries aloud (literally *with my voice*) to God, and God responds. The psalmist may refer to the temple here, or to any high place of sacredness. Mountains have long been seen as divine places. This sacred place reference is continued in the next verse.

Psalm 3:5. The reference to lying down and awakening is perhaps to a period of time spent in the sanctuary, waiting for some word from God.

Psalm 3:6. After the temple night, and because of trust in God, the psalmist reiterates a lack of fear in the face of "tens of thousands drawn up against me."

Psalm 3:7. The psalmist now requests God to "arise." This is the third time the word is used. The enemies have risen (verse 1); but God raises the head of the worshiper (verse 3). Now Yahweh, the God, will arise.

The Hebrew word for *help* and *deliver* are the same. (See verse 2.)

Psalm 3:8. The tone of this psalm is brighter than some of the other laments we will read. There is real confidence that God will right the wrong done to the psalmist. In other laments that confidence is lacking.

Psalm 5. This psalm has a liturgical setting. The psalmist prays in the morning and prepares an appropriate sacrifice in anticipation of God's answer to the prayer. The liturgical setting is confirmed in verse 7 when the psalmist vows to enter God's house, or God's holy temple. Thus, we get a definite setting for the psalm's use in the ancient Israelite religion.

Psalm 5:4-6. Verse 4 describes the psalmist's antagonists in the most general of terms. They are the wicked who do evil. Verse 5 speaks to boasters ("the arrogant") who cannot stand before God. This word is also the word that means *praise* in Hebrew. But its connotation here must be praise of self, or boasting.

The other description of the wicked in verse 5 is more difficult to understand. I have translated it "doers of the uncanny." These wicked ones do mysterious, magical, malicious mischief. They are not only magicians, but they represent any forces opposed to God's righteousness and justice. In verse 6, the wicked are further characterized as liars and people of murder and treachery. Verses 5-6 seem to specify the worst traits of the wicked ones in verse 4. This nasty description is made even more so by verse 9.

Psalm 5:11-12. The righteous are blessed and protected by God, while the wicked will fall and be destroyed.

Psalm 6. The psalm is dominated by the anguished cry, "How long?" In the face of the most appalling troubles, the psalmist is amazed and horrified that God does not respond. And yet, as often in these psalms, the psalmist ends with the affirmation that the God of righteousness will not forever forget the suffering of the righteous worshiper.

Psalm 6:2-3. The phrases here are stock ones, describing a psalmist in serious trouble. Whether the psalmist is bothered by sickness or enemies is not altogether clear in this psalm. "I am faint" more literally would be read "I am cut off." The word *soul* means a person's life force. If there is no soul there is no life. Thus, to say that "my soul is in deep anguish" is to say that death is imminent.

Psalm 6:5. Again we find ourselves struggling with the idea that there is no praise of God in death. This psalmist expects God's intervention into this life to right any wrongs. This verse also serves to motivate that divine intervention. After all, if it can be shown that God's special care for the righteous is not demonstrable to all, dangerous questions about life and its meaning can begin to rise.

Psalm 6:9-10. The holy oracle of the worship service has apparently been given, for the psalmist is now convinced that God "has heard my cry." Doom for the enemies is now assured.

Psalm 7. Nothing is known of Cush, the Benjamite, or this psalm's connection with him.

Psalm 7:3-5. The lament section of this psalm has been replaced by an oath of innocence. The psalmist calls down calamity if he or she has done any of the evil deeds denied in these verses. Many scholars think that the origins of the ritual aspect of this oath of innocence are found in 1 Kings 8:31-32.

Hard cases of justice can in reality only be solved by God. Our psalmist has been accused of some crime or other and has come to the temple to swear an oath disclaiming all wrongdoing. After the oath, God is requested to act in the psalmist's behalf. The longest oath of innocence in the Bible is Job 31. Job claims he has done no crime worthy of the tragedies that have befallen him. He demands a righteous accounting by God and is certain God will find him innocent. The oath prepares Job to meet God. So, after verse 5, the author of Psalm 7 is ready to meet God.

Psalm 7:11. An interesting idea about God is found in this verse. We might read: "God is a righteous judge, / a sentencing God every day." The word translated *wrath* most often means *curse*. The thought of the psalmist is not that God curses the people, but that God judges every day. The sentences God hands down can only be seen as curses to the wicked. The idea of the God of daily judgment is matched by Jesus' famous story of Matthew 25:31-46. Called the parable of the last judgment, it is in reality a parable of daily judgment. Whenever we serve the poor, we serve Christ directly. God is a judge with a daily sentence.

Psalm 7:14-16. These are images that result in malicious comedy. The wicked give birth only to lies and end up being caught in their own traps.

Psalms 9–10. Psalms 9 and 10 are one unit. Together they form an alphabetic acrostic. (See Psalms 34 and 145 for other examples.) They are often thought to be two separate poems, because their context and tone are quite different when taken separately. Psalm 9 sounds like a hymn of praise, while Psalm 10 is a lament. Songs of lament often begin with some sort of laudatory introduction that is in hymn form. Psalms 27, 90, and 139 follow this pattern. Such a hymnlike introduction has a double purpose. First, the hymn is an expression of the enthusiasm and confidence that God will act on behalf of the person who is approaching God.

The psalmist also is trying to induce God to grant the request and so begins with elaborate praise. Appeals to God's honor and to God's obligations in regard to the worshiper's trust are found throughout the psalms.

Psalm 9:3-6. The great deeds of God are described as the defeat of the psalmist's enemies. The enemy has been so utterly annihilated that their very memory has been obliterated.

Psalm 9:7-8. These verses remind us of God as king of the universe, who is to be mirrored in Israel by the earthly king. God, like the visible king, is to establish a throne to judge the world with righteousness and the peoples with integrity and equity. As we saw in the royal psalms, the king's major function in the land was to judge in righteousness and equity.

Psalm 9:12. And God especially, again like the earthly king, hears and never forgets the cry of the afflicted. See also verse 18.

Psalm 9:19-20. The psalm closes powerfully with a call to get clear just who runs the universe. These lines summarize the basic concern of the psalms. All nations and all peoples must stand under God's judgment. All nations and all peoples are humans, not gods. Until they take that fact seriously, the nations will be doomed to turmoil and war.

Psalm 10:1. After the opening hymn to God's power and justice, this second part of the psalm turns to the bold questions of the lament. Given the hymn of Psalm 9, then where is God? Why is God hidden most especially in time of trouble?

Psalm 10:2. The needy, whose hope shall never perish (Psalm 9:18), are now pursued by the wicked. Surely God cannot allow this situation to continue!

Psalm 10:3-11. The psalmist gives us a very dark picture of a world gone mad. The victorious and comfortable wicked man has "no room for God." The evil power seems satisfied and safe. The wicked person, in inner dialogue, claims eternal safety and freedom from all adversity. He lurks in secret to seize the helpless, to capture the helpless in a net (verse 9). Where is the God of the helpless? After another terrible crime, the victim now says, "God will never notice" (in direct contradiction to 9:12) and "[God] *never* sees" (verse 11, italics added).

Psalm 10:12-16. The psalmist now affirms, even though appearances seem otherwise, that God will *not* forget (verse 12, italics added) and that God *does* see (verse 14, italics added). Though the wicked claim that God does not pursue them, the psalmist proclaims that God does precisely that. God is king forever and all nations will perish from the earth.

Psalm 10:17-18. God will hear the concern of the afflicted (*meek*, NRSV) and will do justice to the fatherless and the oppressed. But the persons of the earth will exercise their reigns of terror no more. Psalms 9 and 10 together affirm that God must be praised, worshiped, and believed, particularly at those times when those actions are not easy or obvious.

Psalm 14:1. This rather dark psalm immediately concerns itself with the root cause of human depravity. For the claim that there is no God, the psalmist calls them "fools," a stinging term that indicates a deeply corrupted moral character. The two most famous Old Testament fools were Amnon, David's son, who raped his half-sister, Tamar (2 Samuel 13), and Nabal (his name means "fool"), the husband of Abigail who refused to offer food to David's men.

Those who deny the real existence of God inevitably end up corrupted and do corrupt or abominable deeds. The word translated *corrupt* means "ritually and religiously impure."

Psalm 14:4. Here is a memorable line about naive corruption. All of these evildoers or "doers of the uncanny" (see the discussion of Psalm 5 for this phrase) "devour my people as though eating bread." That phrase sounds contemporary. How many of us blithely consume our huge portions of food, while one billion people starve? Are we devouring people while we devour food? This psalmist, I think, would answer yes.

Psalm 14:7. The psalmist ends by hoping for a complete rebirth of Zion that will lead to the end of practical atheism.

Psalm 22. In many ways, this is the clearest of the lament psalms we have examined thus far. It begins with an address (verse 1) and complaint (verses 1-2). The psalmist then moves to an expression of confidence in God (verses 3-5). This psalm also has an extended request or complaint (verses 12-18. It concludes with a vow of praise (verses 22-26).

Psalm 22:12-18. The most distinctive part of the psalm is found in the colorful request/complaint section. He describes his suffering in images of bulls, lions, and dogs assailing him. His bones pop out of joint, his heart melts, and his tongue sticks to the roof of his mouth. Then some enemies tie him up and gloat over his pitiful physical condition and steal his rag-like clothes.

Psalm 22:22-31. But God answers these sad cries, and the psalmist vows to praise God so forcefully that even subsequent generations will tell of God (verse 30).

The use by two Gospels of the first verse of this psalm is worthy of a few comments. Often Jesus' cry of being forsaken by God is seen purely as one of human despair, and it is partly that. But we need to remember that this lament psalm does not end in despair but ends with God's victory and praise. Could that have been in the minds of Matthew and Mark as they recorded the phrase? Those around the cross think they hear Jesus calling for Elijah, the forerunner of the Messiah. But, as usual in the Gospels, they do not understand Jesus. Did not Mark and Matthew want us to understand that Jesus' cry of dereliction was not only that, but also pointed to an entire psalm that ended in triumph?

DIMENSION THREE: WHAT DOES THE BIBLE MEAN TO ME?

Prayer to God

Discuss with the group the need for honesty in prayer. Real honesty can only happen when we have a real relationship with God, a relationship in the best Old Testament tradition. We must believe that we are very important in God's creation, that God has made us to make a real difference. But also we must believe that God really cares about what we say and do in our lives. With those two ideas in mind we can hear two Old Testament stories that best exemplify the sort of bold piety represented by the psalms of lament.

The first story comes from Genesis 18:22-33. God is going to destroy the wicked Sodom and Gomorrah. But before the sulfur begins to rise, God tells Abraham the plan. Instead of quietly acquiescing to the destructive design of God, Abraham questions God's justice! Abraham haggles with God and forces God to admit that if ten righteous persons can be found in Sodom all the wicked would be spared. After all, Abraham says, "Will not the Judge of all the earth do right?" Here is a bold Abraham indeed!

The second story comes from Exodus 32:7-14. While Moses is up on Mount Horeb/Sinai getting the sacred tablets from God, the people are down at the foot of the mountain having an old-fashioned orgy around the golden calf. God is furious, rejects them all, and shouts at Moses to move out of the way so God can destroy them all and start over again with him. Once again, Moses, like Abraham, does not do just what God wants. In fact, Moses talks God out of it!

Moses uses two arguments. First, the Egyptians will not think of you as much of a God for bringing the Israelites out of Egypt only to destroy them now. Second, have you forgotten your covenant to make the people great and numerous? It is hard to have a numerous people when you destroy all of them except one old prophet. And so, God did not do the evil God was going to do.

These two stories set the stage for the psalms of lament. God hears us. God cares for what we think and do. God wants our honest and heartfelt hurts and joys, pains and triumphs, hatreds and loves. Prayer to God is honest or it is not prayer to God at all.

What would your honest prayer to God be? Can you be honest to God? Why or why not? Do these laments help you reexamine your prayers to God?

"Show me, LORD, my life's end, . . . / let me know how fleeting my life is" (39:4).

INDIVIDUAL LAMENTS

DIMENSION ONE:
WHAT DOES THE BIBLE SAY?

Answer these questions by reading Psalm 27

1. How is the Lord described in this psalm? (27:1)
    The Lord is light, salvation, and a stronghold.

2. What does this psalmist most desire? (27:4)
    The psalmist wants to dwell in the house of the Lord.

3. Who are the enemies of the psalmist? (27:10, 12)
    The enemies are the psalmist's mother and father and other false witnesses.

Answer these questions by reading Psalm 28

4. What is God called? (28:1, 7, 9)
    God is called a Rock, a strength, a shield, and a shepherd.

5. What will God do to the wicked? (28:5)
    God will tear down the wicked and "never build them up again."

Answer these questions by reading Psalm 31

6. What are the two repeated words used to describe God? (31:2, 3)
    God is called rock and fortress twice.

7. Why does the psalmist trust God? (31:15)
    The psalmist believes that his "times are in your [God's] hand."

Answer these questions by reading Psalm 35

8. Who will pursue the wicked adversaries of the psalmist? (35:5-6)

   The angel of the Lord will pursue them.

9. How are the psalmist's enemies described? (35:11)

   They are called ruthless witnesses.

Answer these questions by reading Psalm 38

10. Who has brought on the illness of the psalmist? (38:1-2)

   God has brought the illness ("your arrows have pierced me").

11. How do the friends respond to the illness? (38:11)

   They avoid him and stay far away.

12. How does the psalmist attempt to gain God's help? (38:18)

   The psalmist confesses sin and iniquity.

Answer these questions by reading Psalm 39

13. What does the psalmist want to know? (39:4)

   The psalmist wants to know how fleeting his life is.

14. What is the psalmist's final request to God? (39:13)

   The psalmist wants God to look away from him.

Answer these questions by reading Psalm 42

15. How is the psalmist's desire for God described? (42:1)

   The psalmist longs for God as much as a deer pants for streams of water.

16. What do the men say to the psalmist? (42:3)

   The men say to the psalmist, "Where is your God?"

17. What does the psalmist say to his own soul? (42:11)

The psalmist says, "Why are you downcast and disturbed?"

Answer this question by reading Psalm 43

18. How does the psalmist describe these enemies? (43:1)

The psalmist says these enemies are unfaithful, deceitful, and wicked.

Answer these questions by reading Psalm 51

19. Against whom has the psalmist sinned? (51:4)

The psalmist has sinned against God.

20. What does God require of the psalmist? (51:6)

God desires faithfulness "even in the womb."

21. What does the psalmist ask of God? (51:10)

The psalmist asks for a pure heart and a steadfast spirit.

22. What is an acceptable sacrifice to God? (51:17)

An acceptable sacrifice is a broken spirit and a broken and contrite heart.

DIMENSION TWO: WHAT DOES THE BIBLE MEAN?

The psalms covered in this lesson are Psalms 27, 28, 31, 35, 38, 39, 42, 43, and 51. Psalms 26, 36, 52, and 53 are of the same type, but are not considered in this lesson.

We are confronted in this group of individual laments with tremendous diversity. The Bible does not say the same thing all the time. I find that odd or even dangerous ideas are the very ones we need to look at most closely. If the Bible merely confirms what we already know, then we probably need to read it some more. Some ideas in the Bible simply do not agree with other ideas. We do not study the Bible to find a consistent system of beliefs. We study the Bible to find the vital and living presence of God as clearly as possible. I know of no place in the Bible where God is more vital and alive than in the Psalms.

Psalm 27. Just as in Psalms 9–10, a song of trust and confidence precedes the lament itself in Psalm 27. This is not a sign of the original independence of two poems, but a sign of the freedom of the poet to rearrange and highlight certain parts of given structures.

Psalm 27:1-3. Nothing, not an armed camp, not an erupting war, nor a pack of evildoers can shake the confidence of this psalmist. This statement does not promise the avoidance of trouble. It affirms that during inevitable trouble the resources from God are available to survive the problem. Good Christians are not always safe and happy. This Israelite psalmist agrees with that statement.

Psalm 27:4. The psalmist longs to be in God's house all the days of his life. The similarity to Psalm 23 is really only superficial. In Psalm 23, the psalmist asks to dwell in God's house "for a length of days" (the literal Hebrew). This psalmist wants to dwell there "all the days of my life."

The important difference is found when we ask why the psalmist wants to come to God's temple. Psalm 23 does not raise this question at all. In Psalm 27 (verse 4), the psalmist desires "to envision the splendors of Yahweh, and to inquire in Yahweh's temple" (my translation). The psalmist comes to experience God's splendor, beauty, and delight and to inquire in that temple. The latter task is to discover God's will, to seek the truth of God by means of the ritual.

Psalm 27:6. The vow of praise is couched in promises of a ritual kind. The praise of "shouts of joy" refers to a ritual cry of joy. (See Numbers 23:21; 1 Samuel 4:5; 2 Samuel 6:15; Psalm 33:3.) The singing and chanting ("make music") also have a ritual background.

Psalm 27:7-10. Now the proper address and lament appear. Verse 8 reads literally, "I told you, 'They sought my face.' I seek your face, Yahweh." This translation uses the verb *seek* in two different ways. The enemies sought the psalmist for harm. The psalmist seeks God for aid and goes on to beg God not to "hide your face" from the psalmist (verse 9). A further sign that the psalmist's confidence is unshakable appears when even the psalmist's father and mother abandon the psalmist. Still, the psalmist knows God will gather him up.

Psalm 27:11-14. The psalmist asks for teaching from God to survive the onslaughts of the enemies. The participant book explains the textual problem of verse 13. The psalm ends with the confident psalmist instructing other sufferers to be strong and firm and to wait for God.

Psalm 28:2. Two insights into Israelite worship appear in this verse. The appropriate attitude of prayer in the ancient world, according to texts from both testaments, is to lift hands. Examine, for example, Psalms 63:4; 134:2; 1 Timothy 2:8. A rejection of prayer by God from a sinful people may be found at Isaiah 1:15.

In the second half of the verse, the Hebrew text literally reads, "to your most holy of holies." This refers to the innermost place in the sanctuary, where tradition says that the ark of the covenant could be found.

First Kings 6:16 describes the building of the sacred place, and 1 Kings 8:6-21 tells how the ark was taken into this holy of holies by the priests on the day of the temple's dedication. When the Roman armies sacked Jerusalem in the first century BC, they broke into the most holy place expecting to find the fabled ark of the covenant. Instead, they found nothing at all. The place was empty. The history of the ark of the covenant remains clouded and largely mysterious.

Psalm 28:6. Again we find evidence of some word of assurance coming to the worshiper from the temple liturgy between verses 5 and 6. This remains the most reasonable explanation of the abrupt change of mood from verse 5 to verse 6.

Psalm 28:7-9. The psalm demonstrates how an individual lament could easily have served the communal needs of the entire community. The psalmist first claims God to be a strength and shield, and so gives thanks to God. Then verses 8-9 broaden the praise to the community and to the king. Now God is the strength of the people (verse 8) and a fortress of salvation for the king ("anointed one"). The final cry asks God to save the people and to be their shepherd (verse 9).

God is described as a shepherd in Hosea 4:16, Psalms 23:1, and 80:1. The verse of the Bible that is called to mind by Psalm 28:9 is Isaiah 40:11, a verse made famous by Handel's *Messiah*.

From this shepherd imagery, the New Testament borrows many memorable pictures for its description of Jesus. John 10:1-18 is especially dependent on Jeremiah 23:1-6 and Ezekiel 34 for its imagery.

Psalm 31. This psalm is a classic example of a lament brought about by illness (verses 9-10). The psalmist feels persecuted by arrogant adversaries (verses 4, 18, 20) and shunned by friends (verse 11). The psalmist seeks refuge in God in the face of the possibility of a violent death (verse 13).

Psalm 31:13. The first part of this verse is identical to the first part of Jeremiah 20:10. This fact tells us that the words and phrases of prayers were alive in the traditions of the authors of the Old Testament. Not in every case did they create new words to express thoughts, but they borrowed those that were familiar and powerful. The situation of this psalmist and that of Jeremiah are similar and require a similar response. This example of the living literature of the Bible should teach us that the authors of these texts were not unaware of the traditions that had preceded them. They did not write in ivory towers, but in the midst of life and the literature written to respond to that life.

Psalm 31:21. Again the liturgical oracle has apparently been given between verses 20 and 21. The psalmist proceeds to bless God and to summon others to do the same.

Psalm 35:1. The verb translated contend means "go to court with" and is used often by the prophets in their descriptions of God's "lawsuits" against a sinful Israel. Here the psalmist calls God to be the prosecuting attorney against the enemies of the psalmist.

Psalm 35:2-6. The revenge motif is particularly powerful in these verses and leads to language of violence and bodily injury. Rather than defend this language or explain it away, we should attempt to understand it as the brutally honest expression of a person who feels abandoned, powerless, and terrified. Like a cornered animal, the psalmist lashes out at those who attack.

Psalm 35:20. The phrase "those who live quietly in the land" has evoked much comment among scholars. This is the only time the phrase is used in the Old Testament. Some think it refers to a sect of particularly religious Israelites, separated from the rest of the community. However, the reference is probably metaphorical. The enemies are characterized in the psalm by their evil speaking. In contrast, the psalmist is represented as one of the quiet ones who patiently await God's aid.

Psalm 35:27-28. Then again in contrast to the loud and evil speakers, the formerly quiet one will call on others to shout God's praise, while the psalmist joins in with day-long praise.

Psalm 38. The ancient Christian church listed this psalm among the seven penitential psalms. The others are Psalms 6, 32, 51, 102, 130, and 143. These psalms were found to be particularly expressive of the need for penitence. This penitence would lead, it was hoped, to God's forgiveness. In the psalms, the illness of the sufferer is said to be caused by God.

God is often depicted in the Old Testament as afflicting persons with leprosy or some other particularly horrible disease. (See Exodus 4:6; Numbers 12:9-10; Job 1:11.) God also had smitten the firstborn of Egypt with a plague (Exodus 11:4-5). Israel tended to refer whatever happened, both good and bad, to God. (See Amos 3:6; Isaiah 45:7.)

An even older idea was that illness was a direct outcome of sin. Sin was due to an unrighteous or crooked soul. Perhaps older still is the idea that illness was attributed to demons or evil spirits, either dependent on God or independent of God. (See Exodus 12:23; 2 Samuel 24:16; 2 Kings 19:35.) We have spoken earlier of human beings with malevolent power, who bring on illness. (See my discussion of Psalm 10 in Lesson 7.)

You can see that the Old Testament writers wrestled with the idea of illness and sin. The wrestling does not end with the Old Testament. John 9 raises the issue again. I find Jesus' answer to the question of the disciples in verse 2 especially illuminating. Jesus is saying that God did not cause the blindness, but God will show power in response to the blindness.

Psalm 38:22. No matter how grim the psalmist finds the situation, he does not give up on God. This faith appears to be in sharp contrast to the next psalm.

Psalm 39. This lament has a remarkably independent tone. The only other psalms like this psalm are 73 and 90. The former we will examine in Lesson 12 and the latter in Lesson 11. Each of these poems is more philosophical than emotional in orientation. The enemy is God rather than the wicked, and the problem is mental discomfort or confusion about life's meaning and purpose. The simple solutions of God's automatic reward for the righteous and God's rejection of the wicked are no longer possible in this climate of doubt and difficulty.

Psalm 39:1-3. Rather than have an address to God, the psalmist claims to have kept quiet in the face of God's repeated attacks. The psalmist wants to avoid giving the wicked any comfort and thus soiling the honor of God. This claim is apparently designed to motivate God to solve the problem.

Psalm 39:4-6. But silence is impossible, and a torrent of words accuses God of withholding vital information from the psalmist. The psalmist wants to know how long his life will be. And lying behind the question is the certainty that the length of life is incredibly brief. The words *fleeting*, *handbreadth*, *breath*, and *phantom* make life's brevity all too certain. At the end of verse 6, not only is life short, it is meaningless. One works to gather some goods; but at life's end, no one knows who will take over a lifetime's work.

Psalm 39:7. The psalmist finds hope only in God, accepting the belief that God does all. Only God brings all pain and all joy, and for this psalmist only the former is in evidence.

Psalm 39:9-11. The psalmist declares innocence of the problems he is experiencing; God has done it! The psalmist then asks God to get away and to remove the scourge. God rebukes for sin, but does not know when to stop the punishment!

Psalm 39:12-13. Great anguish is packed into verse 12. God is urged to ease up on the breath-like shadow of a human being. Then, in final despair, the psalmist howls at God to leave him alone. Maybe then a little joy could be gained before death comes.

Psalms 42–43. In this psalm, now artificially appearing as two psalms in our Psalter, we find a powerful literary artist. In a potent metaphor at the beginning, the psalmist establishes in the minds of readers the intent of the entire psalm. The longing tone of the psalmist is thus provided in the clearest of images. The deer panting with thirst is quenched only by the streams of water. The psalmist is quenched only by God.

Psalm 42:3. The question the scorning enemies ask, "Where is your God," is the real question of the psalm.

Psalm 42:4. The answer to the question comes immediately. God is found in the house of God, the Jerusalem temple, where one should go in festival procession. This is the psalmist's obvious goal.

Psalm 42:6-8. God is present in Hermon, near Mount Mizar, an unknown northern mountain of Israel. But God is better found in the temple, as the persistent cry of the psalmist makes manifest.

Psalm 42:10-11. The probing question is asked again. "Where is your God?" But that anguished cry is followed immediately by the repetition of the refrain: "Put your hope in God, / for I will yet praise him."

Psalm 43:4. The psalmist will go to the altar of God and find God there. Then he will praise God there "with the lyre," part of a promised worship experience.

Psalm 43:5. The third use of the refrain (see 42:5, 11) reaffirms the psalmist's certainty that no matter how far from God one finds oneself, either physically or spiritually, hope in God is the cry for all of us. This psalm is certainly one of the finest artistic creations of the Psalter, balanced in structure and linguistic usage.

Psalm 51:1. In this penitential psalm, only God's unfailing love can possibly cleanse the rank sin of this psalmist. The psalmist can only hope for the abundant mercy of God. The word *mercy* is a fascinating and important one. The noun form of this word is translated womb. Thus, at the base of this word for compassion or mercy lies a clearly feminine image. God's love is like the love of a woman for the child of her womb. Women who have given birth can always know more of this understanding of the mercy of God than men can. Thus the conception of God is made the more inclusive and universal.

Psalm 51:4. All sin is ultimately sin against God. You should note how general the understanding of sin is here. The psalm is, because of that fact, not locked into any one time or place. We can make this psalm our own by identifying for ourselves what our sins are.

Psalm 51:7. Hyssop, a thorny plant, refers to a cleansing ceremony. Such a ceremony is found in Exodus 12:22, where hyssop is used to brush the blood onto the doorposts to save the Israelite homes from the destroyer. The cleansing ritual for leprosy employs hyssop (Leviticus 14:4, 6, 48-53). Thus, in the most serious cleansing rituals, hyssop plays a prominent role.

Psalm 51:16-17. External sacrifice is first rejected from a sinful people. All that sinners can offer to God is a broken spirit, that is, a spirit ready to receive God's mercy and be molded to God's will.

Psalm 51:18-19. Nevertheless, in a better society, one more attuned to God, God will accept sacrifice of a physical kind once again.

DIMENSION THREE: WHAT DOES THE BIBLE MEAN TO ME?

Psalms 39, 42, 43—The Diversity of the Psalms

The diversity of the psalms is a reflection of the diversity of Scripture as a whole. The Bible is far less inclined to say the same thing about the same subject as many of its contemporary readers would like to admit. A few examples might be instructive.

Genesis 1 describes a God of awesome majesty who creates by the power of the spoken word. God said, "Let there be light," and light appeared. To a child, this sounds like magic. God is like that in Chapter 1 of Genesis. Poof! Instant world! But in Chapter 2 God has dirty knees and dirt under the fingernails as God kneels in the dirt to mold a human being. The differences are startling. But they capture in the first two chapters of Genesis the remarkable diversity of the pictures of God in the Bible.

The human portrayals are equally amazing. Did you know that all major characters in the biblical witness have some quite negative story told about them, and usually very early in their stories? Noah gets drunk (Genesis 9), Abram lies (Genesis 12), Jacob is deceitful (Genesis 27), Moses is a murderer (Exodus 2), David commits adultery and murder (2 Samuel 11), and Peter is weak and confused (Mark 8; 9; 14). Why is this so? Because the Bible does not present morally perfect human examples. The Bible is a mirror. We look in it and are caught in the glare of our own reflections, both our good sides and our bad sides. It gives moral guidance by demonstrating human need for repentance.

We need to celebrate the Bible's diversity, not try to explain it away. The Bible was written on earth by human beings, themselves from the earth. Bible authors cannot provide absolute authority for us, because God is always revealed to us in and through earthly writings and human beings. None of them can serve as absolute authority. God offers to us our diversity and leaves us with the struggle to work out our faith with "fear and trembling." But God promises to be with us as we struggle. Thus, the authors of Psalms 39 and 42–43 can be helpful to us as we attempt to understand and to live a viable faith in God. We can be grateful to God for God's provision for our freedom to be faithful in the ways we can discover.

Ask whether any member of the class has ever felt like the author of Psalm 39. Ask a class member to recount how she or he felt during those times. Does anyone know other persons who feel this way? How do you respond to such persons out of your own faith? Is Psalm 42–43 a response to Psalm 39?

*Arise to help me; look on my plight! / You, L*ORD* God Almighty, / you who are the God of Israel (59:4-5).*

INDIVIDUAL LAMENTS

DIMENSION ONE:
WHAT DOES THE BIBLE SAY?

Answer these questions by reading Psalm 55
1. What is the psalmist's wish? (55:6-8)
    The psalmist wishes he had wings with which to fly away and find shelter.

2. Who is the psalmist's antagonist? (55:13)
    The antagonist is the psalmist's companion and close friend.

3. What has the antagonist done? (55:20-21)
    The antagonist has violated the covenant by being deceitful.

Answer these questions by reading Psalm 56
4. How does God remember the pains of the psalmist? (56:8)
    God keeps them listed on God's scroll.

5. What will the psalmist do for God? (56:12)
    The psalmist will present thank offerings to God.

Answer these questions by reading Psalm 57
6. How will God save the psalmist? (57:3)
    God will send forth love and faithfulness.

7. How are the psalmist's enemies described? (57:4)

The psalmist's enemies are ravenous beasts with sharp teeth and tongues.

8. What is the psalmist's response to God? (57:7)

The psalmist will be steadfast and will sing and make music to God.

Answer these questions by reading Psalm 58

9. What do the "rulers" do? (58:2)

In their hearts, the rulers devise injustice and mete out violence.

10. When do wicked people become wicked? (58:3)

Wicked people are wicked from the womb (the day of their birth, NRSV).

11. What will the righteous people do when the wicked perish? (58:10)

The righteous will be glad when they are avenged and will dip their feet in the blood of the wicked.

Answer this question by reading Psalm 59

12. What should happen to the wicked? (59:5, 11-13)

The psalmist prays that Go will punish them unsparingly, then relents, claiming that their own sin will eventually consume them.

Answer these questions by reading Psalm 69

13. How does the psalmist describe the problem? (69:1-3)

The psalmist speaks of drowning to describe the problem.

14. What has brought on the psalmist's problems? (69:9)

The psalmist's zeal for the Lord's house has consumed the psalmist.

GENESIS to REVELATION **PSALMS**

15. What have the comforters given to the sufferer? (69:21)

They put gall in his food and gave him vinegar to drink.

Answer this question by reading Psalm 71

16. How long has the psalmist trusted God? (71:5-6)

The psalmist has trusted God from birth.

Answer these questions by reading Psalm 77

17. What is the psalmist's difficult question about God? (77:9)

"Has God forgotten to be merciful?"

18. How does the psalmist think to move beyond despair? (77:11-12)

The psalmist will remember past miracles of God and will meditate on God's works.

19. What historic events does the psalmist remember? (77:16-20)

The psalmist remembers the creation of the world and the Exodus from Egypt.

DIMENSION TWO:
WHAT DOES THE BIBLE MEAN?

The psalms covered in this lesson are Psalms 55, 56, 57, 58, 59, 69, 71, and 77. Psalms 54, 61, 63, 64, and 70 are of the same type, but are not examined in this lesson.

Within these psalms of lament, we will move from a highly individual poem (see Psalm 55) to a song that easily lends itself to the communal worship of Israel (see Psalm 77).

Psalm 55. The psalmist provides us a very human portrait of one who is assaulted and beaten down by antagonists. In response, the psalmist wishes only to fly away.

The word for *dove* in Hebrew (verse 6) is the word *Jonah*, the title of the famous Old Testament book. In that story, God calls Jonah to go to Nineveh, but Jonah, the dove, tries unsuccessfully to fly away from God. In verse 8, the psalmist hopes to find shelter "far from the tempest and storm." "Tempest" and "storm" translate the very same words ("wind" and "storm") used in Jonah to describe God's first attempt to get Jonah to go back on his way to Nineveh (Jonah 1:4). Perhaps the author of Jonah was familiar with Psalm 55 and decided to use this motif of the "fleeing dove" to motivate the plot.

Psalm 55:9-11. The psalmist does not flee, but begins to accuse the enemy of violence and strife in the city. The psalmist calls on God to "confound their words," a reference to the famous story of the tower of Babel (Genesis 11:1-9). This city is infused with destruction, malice, abuse, threats, and lies. These words are a litany of the most terrible of human vices. Surely only God can deal with such a mess!

Psalm 55:12-14. The final and worst problem of all is the deception of the psalmist's familiar friend. One can always avoid one's enemies (verse 12), but the friend is around too much. The word translated "a man like myself" is literally "person as my own way." Everywhere the psalmist goes, the friend can be seen. Especially in worship (verse 14) the friend is there. Formerly a source of comfortable conversation, the friend is now a living mockery of former joy. What is more painful than an unavoidable friend-turned enemy! The psalmist paints a tragically familiar picture here.

Psalm 55:15. This verse is a curse that calls for the enemy to be snatched away alive into Sheol. Perhaps the inspiration for this frightful wish comes from the story of the rebellion of Korah. Korah, along with his entire household, was swallowed alive into Sheol at the command of Moses (see Numbers 16:30-33).

Psalm 55:20-23. The NIV and NRSV assume "my companion" is the subject of verse 20, though the text simply reads "he." Here, the word *covenant* implies the basic human contract between friends. The former friend has trampled on the expectations of real friendship.

The psalmist ends (verse 23) with a steadfast belief in the certain demise of the enemies.

Psalm 56. We really do not know how the psalm titles were created. They are of no historical value whatever. The fact that 2 Samuel 22 is nearly identical to Psalm 18 probably gave the collectors of the psalms the original impetus to attach certain psalms to the biography of David. These attachments could have served two purposes. As the memory of David as the greatest king of Israel grew, it could only serve that memory to have David pray deep-felt poems at significant crisis times in his life. The fact that the author of the Book of Chronicles makes David out to be the originator of worship and music in Israel emphasizes this interest in David as author of many psalms.

After the return of Babylonian exiles (538 BC), the Samaritans boasted that Mount Gerizim was the true sanctuary. David's connection with the psalms could have further insured that Jerusalem, the City of David, was the only true sanctuary.

We should also note that in the Greek translation of the Old Testament (the Septuagint), even more titles are given to psalms than in the Hebrew text. This indicates a growing tendency to specify the psalms' origins and authors in order to increase their authority for the community.

Psalms 56:1-13. The Hebrew text of this psalm appears to be in a very poor condition. That fact should warn us against making too much of the meaning of this psalm. This textual problem is as unfortunate as it is important when we attempt to comprehend the biblical text.

As far as we can tell, the psalm follows a very traditional lament pattern: address, request, complaint, and vow.

Psalm 57:1. Note the similarity in the opening of this psalm to the first verse of Psalm 56. However, there is an important difference in content between the two psalms. In Psalm 56 the psalmist appeals to God's graciousness because of enemies that the psalmist goes on to attack. But in Psalm

57 the appeal to God's mercy is not based on the worshiper's affliction but on trust in God (57:1). This difference in emphasis is important to the tone of the psalm. The tone is remarkably mild for a psalm of lament. It may be that "the shadow of your wings" is a reference to the ark of the covenant where the wings of the cherubim are found. This would mean that the psalmist prays from within the safety of the sanctuary.

Psalm 57:3. Rather than a curse upon the enemies, this psalmist asks for God's love and faithfulness. God's victory over the enemy will not be accomplished through the power of God's weapons of war and anger, but by God's unique divine attributes. Evil is shown to be base in the glaring light of God's holiness. This request is in stark contrast to Psalm 58 that revels in power and destruction.

Psalm 57:4. Though the complaint describes the enemies in the familiar pictures of warriors and lions (see Psalms 10:9; 17:12; 35), the real problem is not war but the power of the word, a very dangerous weapon in human struggles.

Psalm 57:7-10. The vow to praise takes the form of a thanksgiving psalm, bound to the lament that precedes it by verse 6. Verse 6 predicts the demise of the scheming wicked ones. Their death leads inevitably to thanksgiving.

Psalm 57:11. The refrain balances the hymn by repeating verse 5. We thus find four verses of lament, the refrain, the transitional verse 6, four verses of thanksgiving, and the repeated refrain. The psalm is quite obviously an artistic whole.

Psalm 58. The undisguised ferocity of this psalm is to be traced to the very real and ultimate conflict between God and the followers of God (the righteous) and other gods and their followers (the wicked).

Psalm 58:1. The struggle in Israel to determine who was in control of all of life was a bitter one. Every culture that surrounded Israel had a polytheistic conception of divine reality—many gods ruled life. When one thinks of it, that is the logical solution to the problem of understanding the complexity of living. Wind damage was the result of the anger of that god who controlled wind; rain came from the rain god; and so forth.

Israel struggled mightily with an emerging idea that there was only one God in the universe. Various Old Testament texts hint at the belief in many gods (see Psalm 29; 1 Kings 22; Exodus 20:3; Job 1). As the battle progressed, the inevitable question arose about the origins of evil. If one God does all, is that God both good and evil? Psalm 58 seems to point to this struggle—the gods of the wicked (perhaps they are local deities) are eventually vanquished by the only God who judges on earth. The violence of Psalm 58 is engendered by the ultimate combat between the gods and God.

Psalm 58:1-2. Do the gods judge uprightly? After all, the very definition of a God is to be righteous. No, they do not! Quite the contrary, their hands dispense violence, the oppressive evil that is the very opposite of righteousness.

Psalm 58:3-5. Just as the evil gods dole out violence and wrong, so the wicked do on earth. Their evil is forever and unchangeable. Only God can deal with such monstrous wrong.

Psalm 58:6-9. The powerful call to God to institute the curses of these verses may have as its background the legal action described in Deuteronomy 27:11-26. The magic of cursing words is spoken here. God, as judge of the earth, is summoned to make the curses effective.

Psalm 58:10-11. The psalm reaches its bloody, vindictive conclusion, driven by the absolute rejection of all wicked persons and their gods. This is clear evidence in the Old Testament of an intolerant religious fanaticism that cannot be denied. Neither should it be condoned.

Psalm 59. Psalms 57, 58, and 59 have one similar phrase in their headings, "Do Not Destroy." We do not know precisely what is meant by this phrase. It possibly could be musical or thematic or direction to the congregation. However, the three psalms all refer to the treatment of the wicked by God. Psalm 57 says that God will rebuke them with faithfulness and love (57:3). Psalm 58 calls for God's absolute destruction of them (58:10). Psalm 59 seems to suggest both "do not kill" and "do consume" (59:11, 13). Perhaps we are witnessing a theological struggle in these three psalms concerning just what to do with the worshipers outside the Israelite faith who were considered to be pagans. Psalm 75 is the only other psalm that shares this heading with the three psalms under consideration.

Psalm 59:1-5. Verses 1-5 are the usual request for deliverance. This request for deliverance is motivated by the awesome and treacherous enemies and by the worshiper's own conviction of complete integrity (verses 3-4).

"Lord God Almighty, . . . the God of Israel" (verse 5) are divine titles. The literal title "Yahweh of hosts" has always been a confusing one. It occurs more than 250 times in the Old Testament. The word *hosts* has been suggested to refer to Israel's warriors, angels, the stars of the sky, the rival gods and demons subdued by God, and the cherubim above the ark of the covenant. We really have no final way to be certain which of these is implied or intended. We can only be certain that it is a title of majesty, describing God as the leader of a great host, whoever they might be.

Psalm 59:6-7, 14-15. The comparison of the enemies to wild dogs that prowl cities in search of food is a vivid one. If God were simply to slay the wicked, the people might easily forget them and also the power of God. Rather, the psalmist calls on God to make them tremble and to bring them down. Thus, it appears that at the end of verse 11, the wicked remain alive, but defeated, as a living reminder of the final victory of God. But verses 12-13 describe the death of these same wicked. Their death will make it clear to all that God "rules over Jacob" to the ends of the earth.

As I have already indicated, verses 11-13 summarize the two ideas of Psalms 57 and 58 concerning God's dealings with the those consided to be wicked heathens. Could the title used with all of the three psalms, "Do Not Destroy," indicate which way the collectors felt about this issue? We simply do not know.

Psalm 69:1-3. The metaphor of drowning is a vivid one. This metaphor is designed to indicate that the psalmist feels hopeless. The ground under the psalmist has been cut away and only the dangerous flood remains.

Psalm 69:5-6. The psalmist admits sin, and in the admittance, knows that God will always respond to the repentant one. Compare Psalm 59, where the psalmist glories in innocence as the way to insure God's aid.

Psalm 69:7-12. The psalmist suffers but believes that all of the suffering is for the sake of God. The description given is reminiscent of an Old Testament prophet, who speaks the word of God only to be rebuffed by the people. The rejection of the psalmist is complete. The psalmist is rejected by his brothers (verse 8), the legal court (verse 12), and even the drunkards who lie at the city gates (verse 12).

Psalm 69:13. The psalmist very humbly asks God to answer at an acceptable time. The psalmist means that the answer will come when God chooses to offer it, at a time favored by God.

Psalm 69:22-28. Terrible curses are uttered out of desperation against the enemy.

Psalm 69:30-31. Again the theme appears that God desires songs of thanksgiving rather than animal sacrifice.

Psalm 69:32-33. Those who especially need the word of God's deliverance and salvation will hear it. The poor, the needy, and the "captive people" are always the groups especially cared for by God.

Psalm 71:5-6. The psalmist's age leads him to turn to the past and his long trust in God as the way to motivate the intervention of God.

Psalm 71:7-11. Verse 7 reads "I have become like a portent to many" (NRSV). The word *portent* in English has the connotation of an evil event that is forthcoming. This is not what the text intends. The psalmist proclaims to God that he has been a good sign (see NIV), a beacon light to many, because of continual praise of God (verse 8). The psalmist then urges God not to "cast me away" in the time of old age.

Psalm 71:17-19. The psalmist insists that old age simply affords a deeper experience of God. The psalmist can now powerfully be proclaimed "to a generation, to anyone who comes" (a literal rendering of the Hebrew).

Psalm 71:20. The psalmist speaks metaphorically. At times, old age felt like death, but the power of God revived the psalmist, and more than once.

Psalm 77. The problem of the psalm is clearly the affliction of the whole people. This has moved the psalmist to ask those probing questions of God that Israel often asked in times of great crisis. (See especially Lamentations 5:20-22, the despairing response to the destruction of Jerusalem by the Babylonians.)

Psalm 77:1-9. These verses are the lament of the psalm. The psalmist is in agony, because God is nowhere to be found in the midst of the current trouble. In verses 5-6, the psalmist attempts to muse on the problem, to meditate about it. The result of the meditation is the series of brooding questions of verses 7-9. (See also Psalms 74:1; 79:5; 80:4.)

Psalm 77:10. This is the psalm's key verse. The psalmist now discovers the real reason why it is impossible to move beyond the brooding questions of verses 7-9. The psalmist realizes that his problem is that the right hand of the Most High has changed. This statement testifies to an important fact. The history of the world can reveal God, but can also obscure God.

The psalmist wanted to force God into a familiar pattern of behavior. To the psalmist now, however, it appears that God has changed. But in reality, God has not changed. The psalmist's perception of God needs to change if God's new activity is to be recognized.

Psalm 77:11-15. When the psalmist meditated on a narrow expectation of God (verse 6), the result was despair. Now the psalmist turns to the works of God, works in history. These are works with a rather mysterious cast.

Psalm 77:16-20. The psalmist turns to an ancient creation hymn to describe the power of God. Genesis 1 is the inspiration for it, but see also Judges 5:4-5. The key verse is "Your way was through the sea; / your path through the mighty waters; / but your footprints were not seen" (my translation).

God operated, but mysteriously, in an unseen way. The psalmist's meditation on the ancient works of God has led to a deeper insight into God. God is not confined to the obvious but can be seen in the unseen, and while unseen appears in the seen. Thus, Psalm 77 is a profoundly theological psalm.

DIMENSION THREE: WHAT DOES THE BIBLE MEAN TO ME?

Psalm 58 —God's Vengeance

In your discussion of this troublesome topic, you should always emphasize that the Bible's use of the word *vengeance* very seldom carries with it the idea of vindictiveness or revenge. In fact, the most recent work on the biblical word usually translated *vengeance* or *revenge* indicates that such a translation is misleading. The word is used in the context of a request to a faithful sovereign to rescue a faithful subject. This would of necessity involve the defeat or punishment of the offending party. But, we should think less of revenge than of the securing and vindicating of the community. In other words, the revenge is rather the restoration of the *shalom* of the community.

When in Psalm 58 the "righteous will be glad when they are avenged," what is meant is that the righteous will witness the defeat of the false gods of verse 1. They will see the vindication of the righteous community. This, of course, does not explain away the gloating fury of the righteous in the psalm. But we do know that such gloating was a problem to the earliest Jewish communities. An old Jewish *haggadah* will illustrate this fact.

Very early in Jewish history it became the custom to tell a story (*haggadah*) to expand on and to illuminate biblical texts. I will tell an early *haggadah* about the great victory at the Red Sea. After the Egyptians were drowned in the sea, and the Israelites had passed over on dry ground, Miriam led the Israelite choir in a rousing chorus of "O for a Thousand Hebrew Tongues to Sing." (It is permissible to embroider your *haggadah* a bit.) Well, they got so carried away, so boisterous and so loud, that the sound carried all the way to heaven; so the angels, who were bored, picked up the enthusiasm of the song and joined in, dancing, laughing, and singing all at the same time. Suddenly from the highest heaven a huge voice boomed out. "You dare to sing while my children are drowning?" And the singing stopped, but the drowning didn't.

This early tale (perhaps from the fourth century AD) indicates that vengeance in the sense of punishment and rescue may happen in the Bible. But there can never be room for gloating, for vindictiveness, or for revenge. "Vengeance is mine, says God."

Are there other Bible passages dealing with these issues that trouble you? Which ones are they, and how do you understand them? Has this discussion been helpful to you?

Close the session by reading together the famous benediction from Numbers 6:24-26. But extend its meaning to all of God's children everywhere.

*Out of the depths I cry to you, L*ORD *(130:1).*

INDIVIDUAL LAMENTS

DIMENSION ONE: WHAT DOES THE BIBLE SAY?

Answer these questions by reading Psalm 88

1. Where does the psalmist draw near? (88:3)

The psalmist draws near to the grave (Sheol).

2. Does God remember the dead? (88:5)

God does not remember the dead.

3. Does the psalmist have any hope? (88:13-18)

No, the psalmist can find no hope.

Answer these questions by reading Psalm 94

4. How is God described? (94:1)

God is a God who avenges.

5. What do the wicked do? (94:5-7)

The wicked crush, oppress, slay, murder, and taunt.

6. Who rises up against the wicked? (94:17)

God rises up against the wicked.

Answer these questions by reading Psalm 102

7. What are the days of the psalmist like? (102:3)

The days vanish like smoke.

8. What will cause future generations to praise God? (102:19-20)

God will hear the prisoner's groans and release the dying.

9. What will finally perish? (102:25-26)

The foundations of the earth and the heavens will finally perish.

Answer these questions by reading Psalm 108

10. Why will the psalmist sing praise? (108:4)

The psalmist will sing praise because God's great love is higher than the heavens.

11. What is Moab to God? (108:9)

Moab is God's washbasin.

12. Who will trample down the psalmist's foes? (108:13)

God will trample down the foes.

Answer these questions by reading Psalm 109

13. What does the psalmist receive in return for love? (109:5)

The psalmist receives evil for good and hatred for friendship.

14. What does the psalmist want to happen to those who curse? (109:17)

The psalmist wants them to be cursed.

15. What is the psalmist's condition? (109:22-25)

The psalmist is poor and needy, his heart is wounded, his knees are weak, his body is gaunt.

Answer these questions by reading Psalm 120

16. Where does the psalmist live? (120:5)

    The psalmist lives in Meshek and Kedar.

17. What does the psalmist want? (120:7)

    The psalmist wants peace.

Answer these questions by reading Psalm 130

18. Where is the psalmist located? (130:1)

    The psalmist is in the depths.

19. If God counted sins, who could stand? (130:3)

    If God kept a record of sins, no one could stand.

20. For whom should Israel hope? (130:7)

    Israel should put their hope in God.

Answer these questions by reading Psalm 139

21. What has God done to the psalmist? (139:1-3)

    God has searched and known the psalmist and is totally familiar with him.

22. Where can the psalmist flee from God's presence? (139:7-12)

    There is no place for the psalmist to flee from God's presence not heaven, the depths (Sheol), the dawn, the far side of the sea, or the darkness.

23. What did God do originally for the psalmist? (139:13)

    God created his inmost being and knit the psalmist together in his mother's womb.

DIMENSION TWO:
WHAT DOES THE BIBLE MEAN?

The psalms to be covered in this lesson are 88, 94, 102, 108, 109, 120, 130, and 139. Psalms 86, 140, 141, 142, and 143 are of the same type, but are not considered in this lesson.

The fact that these psalms are so diverse is important. Unless we can include within our religious lives the diversity of our whole lives we run the danger of compartmentalizing religion. Religion has become for many a nice thing one does on Sunday before turning on the television or starting the first project. The psalms demonstrate with power and clarity that all of life, the shabby and the pretty, is included in God's plan and thus should be included in our religious lives. That diversity is no better demonstrated than in this lesson, as it moves from Psalm 88 to Psalm 139. Help class members wrestle with this diversity and with their diversity as you read these psalms.

Psalm 88:3-7. The word translated *troubles* in verse 3 is usually translated *evils*. Given the fact that the psalmist straightforwardly blames God for his ills, *evils* is a better reading here. Verses 5-6 provide us with another description of the Hebrews' understanding of Sheol, the place of the dead. (See also verses 10-12; Job 10:21-22; and Isaiah 38:18-19.) The dead are cut off from God forever. Verse 5 expresses this terrible fact by saying God remembers them no more.

Psalm 88:9. It is not because the psalmist has not prayed that God has forgotten. The psalmist has cried to God every day, spreading out his hands in the attitude of prayer. Daily prayer is no guarantee of happiness or good health, says Psalm 88.

Psalm 88:10-12. These verses are tremendously pessimistic. All of the ways that God is known are said not to exist in the grave (Sheol). God does not perform wonders there. There is no praise of God. No one there knows or relates God's love or faithfulness. Not to know these facets of God is not to know God at all. Thus, God's righteousness, that is, God's concern for equity and shalom, is not available in Sheol. The psalmist is saying to God, "If I die, you and I are separated forever."

Psalm 88:13-18. The prayer of the psalmist continues, but the silence of God also continues. All have abandoned the psalmist, both on earth and in heaven. As the psalm ends, the despair deepens, and the agony is not assuaged.

Psalm 94. This poem seems originally to have been an individual prayer (see verses 16-23). But the rather general description of the wicked makes it easily adaptable to congregational use.

Psalm 94:1-3. These verses set the desperate tone of the psalm. The psalmist calls for God to arise and cleanse the earth of wickedness, to bring sense and wholeness back to a world apparently gone mad. The anguished question of verse 3 is the question of every age. In a world created good by God how is it that the wicked so often triumph? How does God deal with the wicked? Is there a time when the wicked are paid back for all their evil? This difficult question led to speculation about the "day of God," a time when God would right all the sins of the earth. This psalm affirms that God does avenge the righteous against the wicked. The question later became, "when?"

Psalm 94:4-7. The facts concerning the actions of the wicked are terrible to behold. The worst that is said of them is in verse 6. The treatment of widows and the fatherless is the way any society is judged concerning its righteousness. By including the foreigner (alien, NIV 1984; stranger,

NRSV), the psalmist simply increases the indictment against the wicked. A foreigner or sojourner in the Old Testament can be defined as a person who has been forced to leave his original place or tribe because of war, famine, or other misfortunes. As a result of being a stranger, the foreigner has curtailed civil rights of property, marriage, participation in worship, and the administration of justice.

The verb translated *murder* is the verb used in the two listings of the Ten Commandments, Exodus 20:13 and Deuteronomy 5:17. It implies killing that does not pertain to capital punishment or war (both practiced by the Hebrews).

Psalm 94:8-11. The psalmist attacks anyone who believes that God is incapable of dealing with the wicked. The nonbelievers are fools and dullards. The psalmist argues that God is far greater than human beings. God plants and forms the eyes and ears, and also chastens nations. Human thought, on the other hand, is futile.

Psalm 94:12. God disciplines, or teaches, by suffering, says the psalmist. The psalmist goes on to argue that we should be happy to receive such discipline. In effect, the psalmist implies that the suffering endured by the righteous at the hands of the wicked is done to teach and should be accepted.

Psalm 94:15. Such righteous suffering cannot continue for long, because that is not the way the world or God is. The psalmist remains convinced that God will bring the triumph of righteousness.

Psalm 102. This psalm is another example of an individual poem being adapted for communal use.

Psalm 102:1-11. The psalmist appears to describe illness in ways we have heard before. The lament and address (verses 1-2) are quite traditional.

Psalm 102:12-22. But now the lament is uttered on behalf of a captive Jerusalem. The Lord "will arise and have compassion on Zion" and then "will rebuild Zion." The individual lament has been taken up into the national concern of the nation Israel. The ill health of the individual sufferer has been reinterpreted as the ill health of the nation. In response to the national sickness, God looks down from the holy height and hears the groans of prisoners. God set free those doomed to die. God will act on behalf of Jerusalem/Zion, affirms the psalmist.

Psalm 102:23-24. Even when the psalmist appears to revert to the individual lament, this ill can apply to the nation.

Psalm 102:25-27. The psalmist closes by proclaiming that all of this suffering, indeed the very heavens and earth, will pass away, while God will endure always. (See Isaiah 43:10, 13, 25 for a similar thought.)

Psalm 108. This psalm is a creation out of two pieces of other psalms. It would be valuable to see how different the pieces are in their other contexts.

Psalm 108:1-5 equals Psalm 57:7-11. In Psalm 57, the piece follows bitter lament and thus serves as a vow of praise, a hopeful piece after much despair. In Psalm 108 it begins the psalm, emphasizing more strongly the mood of exultation. This psalm does not have any mood of despair!

Psalm 108:6-13 equals Psalm 60:5-12. Also in Psalm 60, this piece follows a bitter lament against God who has "rejected us" (verse 1). No God speaks in the sanctuary to deny rejection. On the contrary, God lays claim to a territory equal to or greater than what Israel had at its most prosperous time under the Davidic United Monarchy.

In Psalm 108 the piece now emphasizes that God's great love (verse 4) has been made manifest by God's victory over the nations. Only verse 11 has a moment's lament, quickly swallowed up by the strong affirmation of God's power that will trample down our enemies (verse 13). Thus, two answers to laments in Psalms 57 and 60 are joined together to create a victory song. The lament is overshadowed by the power of God.

Psalm 109. Attempting to be very specific about the actual background of a psalm is risky. The psalms are to be used in worship and are not often clearly autobiographical. But Psalm 109 does appear to provide for us a rather clear picture of a person who has been accused of a crime. The psalmist proclaims innocence, laments an illness brought on by the accusation, prays that those accusations may fall on the heads of the accusers, and finally praises God for certain salvation. The psalmist trusts that God is with the needy and those condemned to death.

Psalm 109:1-5. The psalmist rejects the accusations of the "lying tongues." The psalmist has offered only love and has been falsely accused of a foul deed.

Psalm 109:6-19. The psalmist here probably is repeating before God the accusations hurled by the enemies. Verse 6 is best translated: "Seek a wicked one against him! / Let an accuser stand at his right hand!" (my translation). These must be words spoken by the psalmist's enemies, now repeated by the psalmist. The word *accuser* is *satan* in Hebrew. Here, as in Job, it is strictly a legal term. It could also read *prosecuting attorney*. Verse 16 implies that the accusers accuse the psalmist of injustice, a typical charge. But verse 17 sounds like the charge of sorcery, a very dangerous one in ancient Israel.

Psalm 109:20-27. The false accusations have taken their toll on the psalmist. The psalmist is diseased and rejected by all.

Psalm 109:30-31. The psalmist now identifies himself with the needy. The psalmist is still convinced that God will come and right this foul misapplication of justice.

Psalm 120:2. Once again, lying and deceit are prominent in the psalm. The problem has to do with verbal disagreements, false accusations, or cursing hatred. This question of truth-telling was such a crucial element for society that it appears as the ninth commandment. If there is no truth-telling someplace in society, then there can be no society. Only God can be the final arbiter of truth.

Psalm 120:3-4. Lying and deceit should be treated with sharp arrows and burning coals. In other words, liars should be slaughtered and incinerated.

Psalm 120:5-6. Meshek lies somewhere between the Black Sea and the Mediterranean Sea, north and somewhat west of Israel in Asia Minor. Kedar is said to be a tribe of Bedouins in the Syrian-Arabian desert, somewhat east and south of Israel. Thus, the places are remote and wild and probably are not the actual dwelling places of the psalmist. The fact that they are hundreds of miles apart lends support to the supposition that the psalmist is speaking figuratively here. The chief characteristic of these two places is that they "hate peace."

Psalm 120:7. This verse is literally: "I am peace, but when I speak, / they are for war." The psalmist embodies peace and really lives peace, while the remote places are warlike.

Psalm 130. This psalm is the classic penitential psalm, quite often linked to Psalm 51. It demonstrates in an almost tangible way the movement of the penitent from the depths (verse 1) to the redemption of God (verse 8).

Psalm 130:1. The depths are a symbol of the psalmist's enormous separation from God, both physically and spiritually.

Psalm 130:3. The psalmist admits that sin is the cause of unhappiness. If God kept account according to merit, no one could survive the accounting. The belief in justification by faith, not works, is emphasized.

Psalm 130:4. Just as surely as the psalmist knows the depths of his sin, the psalmist also knows that the forgiveness of God more than matches the great depths of wickedness.

Psalm 130:5-6. Still it is hard to wait, and the psalmist often asks the question, How long? Here the psalmist emphasizes the anxiety of waiting by repeating the word wait. The sighing, longing quality of the Hebrew text is hard to capture in a translation. Thirty-six words of English are needed to translate only six in Hebrew.

Psalm 130:7-8. Though the wait is long and difficult, the psalmist waits in confidence and assurance, because unfailing love and full redemption are hallmarks of God. The word translated redemption is originally a legal term that means "to purchase, to offer in exchange for." In the place of the longing soul, chained in the depths, God will offer unfailing love. This will be done for all individuals.

The same redemption will be given to Israel for all its iniquities. One gets the impression of a profound religious experience here. Isaiah, the prophet, had a similar experience. When confronted by God he felt he was a man of unclean lips, who lived among a people of unclean lips. (See Isaiah 6.) This psalmist knows that individual redemption must be matched by a national redemption. The psalmist is in solidarity with the people.

Psalm 139. One must be careful not to ask the questions of this psalm in the wrong way. Psalm 139 is not a contemplation of eternity by an ivory tower theologian. A very definite and real worshiping situation called this psalm to be written. The reason that God's omniscience and omnipresence are spoken of is to motivate God to intervene in the situation of lament.

Psalm 139:1-6. The psalmist is writing theologically here, but it is theology of a very personal kind. The psalmist does not describe an abstract God of omniscience. God has searched and known the psalmist. God knows the ways of the psalmist. And the psalmist ends the description of God's knowledge with the humble admission that such incredible knowledge cannot be attained by a human. This statement reminds one instantly of Genesis 3 where the human beings attempt to gain the knowledge that the serpent promised would make them Godlike. This psalmist knows that the knowledge of God is beyond us.

Psalm 139:7-12. God is everywhere. Nothing bars God's presence, not even the depths/Sheol. As we have seen several times (Psalms 115 and 88, for example), the idea that God is capable of being in Sheol is quite different from other ideas of the power of Sheol. This view of the God who is even in Sheol was formulated by a lamenting psalmist, not a philosopher. This psalmist knew that God's power and presence had to be unlimited if the psalmist were to survive the suffering he was facing.

Unless the power of God is power for us, then all the abstract belief in the world means precisely nothing. Unless I know God is for me, then hours of reading about God or listening about God are only intellectually interesting, but spiritually wasted. The question we must ask is not, Who is God?, but Who is God for me?

Psalm 139:16. This verse has been interpreted as a statement of predestination—God has established the life of the psalmist before his actual body even appeared in the mother's womb (verse 13). The translation is here quite difficult, but the sense seems to be roughly as the text has it. Rather than an abstract statement of a doctrine of predestination, the psalmist graphically states the belief that God's will overshadowed his life from the very beginning. This statement sounds similar to Jeremiah when the prophet records his call to prophesy and Paul when he claims his conversion was in God's plan for him from the beginning. (See Jeremiah 1:5 and Galatians 1:15.) The awesome view of God held by all three of these authors leads them to their claims of God's overwhelming providence.

Psalm 139:19-22. The awesome God of this psalm will not allow wickedness to continue. The psalmist is allied with God against any who would dare oppose God. These verses provide the reason for the theology of verses 1-18. Without the lament, no profound theology can appear.

Psalm 139:24. "Ancient way" is a better translation of the Hebrew than "everlasting." The psalmist asks for God to lead in the way tried and true, the way that leads to righteousness, not wickedness.

DIMENSION THREE: WHAT DOES THE BIBLE MEAN TO ME?

Psalms 88 and 139—The God of the Psalms

The God of the psalms is the God of the Bible. The enormous diversity of the portraits of God in the psalms is matched by a similar diversity in the Bible as a whole. Recognizing and embracing this diversity can help us appreciate and celebrate the freedom of God. A God who is truly free is a God who can be present in even the most unexpected ways, even in the dark mystery of Psalm 88.

The best story I know about the freedom of God comes from one of the most influential theologians of the twentieth century, Karl Barth. Barth was the coauthor of the famous *Barmen Declaration* of 1932. This declaration said, in effect, that Hitler was not the head of the church and that National Socialism was completely incompatible with Christianity. For his labors, he was expelled from Germany and spent the remainder of his life in Basel, Switzerland. He came to the United States on a lecture tour in 1965, three years before his death. From 1932 until 1962 he wrote an enormous study of theology entitled *Church Dogmatics,* a multivolume work, running thousands of pages and addressing a broad range of theological topics.

After a lecture an American reporter asked Barth to give in a brief form his understanding of the nature of God. Barth thought a moment and said, "I have this recurring dream. I dream I die and go on my way to heaven, pushing a wheelbarrow full of my books; there are too many to carry, you know. I amble past St. Peter, who mutters something like 'Well done.' Then I am escorted into the presence of God. God looks at me, cocks a great divine eyebrow, and with a slight smile says, 'No, you're wrong!'"

That is what I mean about the freedom of God. Even the great Barth knew that God was far more than his human words could encompass. And that is the God of the psalms. God is here, but elusive. God is revealed but is also mysterious. God is light and life, but sometimes dark and absent. This is our God! Celebrate such a God who goes beyond any sense of our control of God's actions or thoughts!

Ask class members to reflect on these questions. Is your God free? Or do you try to limit God to behavior that you can understand and accept? Does the diversity of the psalms help you to see God in new ways? How?

By the rivers of Babylon we sat and wept (137:1).

11
COMMUNAL LAMENTS

DIMENSION ONE:
WHAT DOES THE BIBLE SAY?

Answer these questions by reading Psalm 12

1. How does the psalmist describe the rest of humanity? (12:1-2)

   The faithful have vanished; everyone else is a liar and a deceiver.

2. What does the psalmist hope the Lord will do? (12:3-4)

   The psalmist hopes the Lord will cut off their flattering lips and boasting tongues.

3. How does the psalmist describe God's promise? (12:6)

   The psalmist says God's promises are flawless as purified (refined) silver.

Answer these questions by reading Psalm 44

4. What has the psalmist heard about God? (44:1-3)

   The psalmist has heard of the deeds God did in the days long ago.

5. In what does the psalmist not trust? (44:6)

   The psalmist does not trust in bow or sword.

6. Why does Israel "face death all day long"? (44:22)

   Israel faces death for God's sake.

Answer these questions by reading Psalm 74

7. What does the psalmist ask God to remember? (74:2)

> *God is asked to remember the congregation and Mount Zion ("the people of your inheritance" and the tribe "whom you redeemed").*

8. What have God's enemies done to the sanctuary? (74:7)

> *They have burned the sanctuary to the ground.*

9. On what fact of God's history does the psalmist rely? (74:12-17)

> *God has created the universe.*

Answer these questions by reading Psalm 80

10. How is God described in the first verse? (80:1)

> *God is the "Shepherd of Israel."*

11. How is Israel described? (80:8-13)

> *Israel is compared to a vine carefully tended.*

Answer these questions by reading Psalm 83

12. What are the enemies saying in this psalm? (83:4)

> *They want to destroy the nation of Israel.*

13. Which groups have made alliance against Israel? (83:6-8)

> *Edam, Ishmaelites, Moab, Hagrites, Byblos, Ammon, Amalek, Philistia, Tyre, and "even Assyria" have formed an alliance against Israel.*

Answer these questions by reading Psalm 90

14. How long has God been God? (90:2)

> *God has always been God from "everlasting to everlasting."*

15. What are one thousand years in God's sight? (90:4)

    One thousand years are as a day "just gone by" to God.

16. How long does the psalmist claim to live? (90:10)

    The psalmist assumes he will live seventy years, eighty if given special strength.

Answer these questions by reading Psalm 126

17. What happened when the Lord brought back the captives to Zion? (126:2)

    The people were filled with laughter and songs of joy.

18. What does the psalmist want God to do? (126:4)

    The psalmist wants God to restore their fortunes.

Answer these questions by reading Psalm 137

19. Where is the psalmist writing the psalm? (137:1)

    The psalmist writes by the rivers of Babylon.

20. What did the oppressors ask of the captives? (137:3)

    They asked them to sing one of the songs of Zion.

21. What would make the psalmist happy with regard to Babylon? (137:8-9)

    The psalmist praises as happy anyone who dashes Babylonian infants against rocks.

DIMENSION TWO: WHAT DOES THE BIBLE MEAN?

The psalms for this lesson are Psalms 12, 44, 74, 80, 83, 90, 126, and 137. Psalms 60, 79, 85, 123, 125, and 129 are of the same type, but are not examined in this lesson. These psalms represent responses to crises. Here the community is in crisis. How can their responses be useful to us as we respond to our crises?

Psalm 12. This lament takes the form of a complaint against the general evil of the time, particularly lying and boasting (verses 1-4). In the worship service, the word of God's protection is given (verse 5). In verses 6-8, the community responds to the protection of God by affirming God's trustworthiness and compassion. This liturgy of the oppressed may be compared to Isaiah 33, a prophetic liturgy where Babylon is seen as the enemy.

Psalm 12:1-2. External enemies are not the problem here. The generation of the psalmist's people are all wicked. This, of course, implies that the psalmist is not wicked. The word translated lies is the same word used to prohibit empty oaths in the Ten Commandments (Exodus 20:7). Thus, verse 2 of the psalm appears to mean that the society of the psalmist is characterized by lies in legal settings. If truth-telling is not found in court, there can be no truth anywhere. If lying persists, society is doomed. *Deception* (verse 2) is rendered "a double heart" in the New Revised Standard Version. The Hebrew term for double heart is "heart and heart." This is similar to our phrase, "speaking out of both sides of one's mouth." It is a vivid image of hypocrisy.

Psalm 12:3-4. These oath-breakers and hypocrites not only do these foul deeds, they actually boast about them! As long as they have their flattering lips, they say, they are unconquerable. Only God can finally unmask the hypocrite, who is always protected by a rain of words.

Psalm 12:5. The priest or prophet apparently utters the word of God's intention to come and save the sufferer. The psalmist now describes himself as "poor" and "needy." These terms do not describe economic poverty, but contrast the psalmist to the ungodly, who show no need of God.

Psalm 12:6-8. In a world where the wicked "freely strut about" (verse 8), God's words (promises) are certain. They are purer than purified (refined) silver. In worship, the sufferer can be certain that God will protect us from those around us.

Psalm 44. This psalm bears many affinities with the Book of Deuteronomy. That book has been unfairly judged by some as a book of legalism. Nothing could be further from the truth. In Deuteronomy, we find a series of sermons based on the history of Israel that highlight the love and power of God. Psalm 44:1-3 is reminiscent of Deuteronomy 8:17.

Psalm 44:1-3. Israel won great victories in the past, but those victories were never the result of the people's own strength. The victories were God's doing because God "loved them." (See Deuteronomy 7:7-8 for this idea.) God's love preceded God's choosing and God's law. These verses and the entire Book of Deuteronomy are both accounts of God's wonderful and mysterious grace.

Psalm 44:4-8. God loved that community in the past and gave them victories. God will do the same for the psalmist's community. As a result, this community will affirm that they have not won a victory. God has done it all. These verses show how the psalms make new the old traditions. Here the psalmist makes alive for community the interpretation of God's ancient activity.

Psalm 44:9-16. Though the psalmist claims that God has acted in victory and will act in victory, the Israelites have suffered a crushing defeat (verse 10). Some scholars, on the basis of verse 11, believe this poem was written after the Babylonian Exile (after 587 BC). That was the time when Israel was in truth "scattered . . . among the nations." But laments are often exaggerated to deepen the impression of the anguish. Thus, we should avoid assigning any particular history to this psalm. Defeat came often for Israel and this psalm speaks to it.

Psalm 44:17-22. Israel should be constantly victorious. They have not turned from God nor have they forgotten either God or the covenant. If Israel had forgotten, would not God have discovered it (verse 21)? But no. The psalmist cries that their defeat is exactly "for [God's] sake" (verse 22). The psalmist sees even the terrible defeat as part of God's desire for Israel, even though the reason for it is unknown. In this spirit, Paul puts this haunting phrase in the midst of his most powerful and memorable statement about the love of God. (See Romans 8:35-39.)

Psalm 44:23-26. The anguish and bitterness of the cry for help that closes the psalm emphasizes the desperation of the situation. (Compare Psalm 78:65 and Isaiah 51:9 for similar talk of the awakening of God.)

Psalm 74. Connecting this psalm with the destruction of the Jerusalem temple by Babylon in 587 BC is very tempting. However, verse 9 states that "no prophets are left." We know that at the time of the temple's burning two of Israel's most famous prophets, Jeremiah and Ezekiel, were at the height of their prophecy. The reference to the lack of a prophet could mean prophets who worked for the temple, but we can hardly be certain. Verse 4 states that the enemies have "set up their standards as signs." This could refer to the pagan sacrifice performed by Antiochus IV on the Jerusalem altar in 167 BC. But we do not know for sure. Psalm 74, as most psalms, is hardly bound to one time and place.

Psalm 74:1-2. The burning of the Jerusalem temple was the darkest hour of Israel's history. The king, the priesthood, and the promise of God's presence were all wrapped up in the temple. All of these disappeared for many when the temple was destroyed. For this reason, the opening question of the psalm is sharp and pointed: "O God, why have you rejected us forever?" The word translated rejected is later used by the author of the Chronicles to describe the removal of a bad priest from office. (See 2 Chronicles 11:14. For other uses of the same word, see 1 Chronicles 28:9 [reject], 2 Chronicles 29:19 [removed].) Thus, God has in effect fired Israel from the job of being chosen; how else could one explain the end of the temple?

Psalm 74:3-8. The psalmist describes the temple's end in bitter and morbid detail. The intruders break in and set up their own standards or religious signs as emblems of victory (verse 4). Verses 5-6, a terrible mess in the Hebrew text, suggest hammering and smashing. After this brutal assault, they set the building on fire and burn it to the ground (verse 7). Then they rush out to burn any other divine meeting places in the country.

Psalm 74:9-11. Because the enemy's "signs" are more visible, the Israelites can no longer see their "miraculous signs." This could also mean that the givers of signs, the priests, are gone. And so, without priest, prophet, or wise person to ask the questions and to provide some answers, the psalmist picks up the cry, "How long?" (verse 10).

Psalm 74:12-17. At that point a remarkable thing happens. The apparently dispirited psalmist returns in faith to the oldest story of Israel's divine history, the creation of the world. And the story is told in its very oldest guise, complete with ancient mythological references to the combat tales of long ago. Just as God originally crushed the heads of Leviathan, so the psalmist hopes God will crush the heads of the new dragons of chaos, the enemies who have sacked the temple. No clearer example of how the ancient story is made contemporary can be offered than this one.

Psalm 74:18-23. With God's power clearly affirmed and publicly proclaimed, the community calls out with renewed power. They ask God to come once again to defeat the forces of evil. Since God has done it before, let God do it again!

Psalm 80:1-3. This psalm probably comes from the northern traditions of a divided Israel. The Joseph tribes, Ephraim, Benjamin, and Manasseh, are clearly identified with that part of the country. Also, the traditions of the ark of the covenant are usually considered to be northern. (The phrase "enthroned between the cherubim" refers to the ark.) This lament, directed at God, may come from around the time of the Northern Kingdom's destruction by the Assyrians in 721 BC. God is apparently angry "against the prayers of your people" (verse 4). Psalm 78:67-68 also uses a tradition wherein God rejects the northern Joseph group, but loves the southern Judah group. David came from Judah.

Psalm 80:4-7. That the Israelites weep and the enemies scorn and laugh is a very common theme in many communal laments.

Psalm 80:8-13. This parable of Israel as the vine should be compared with Isaiah 5:1-7, another extended example of the same metaphor. Note the differences. In Isaiah, God plants the vineyard expecting a great and sweet harvest, but instead gets wild, bitter grapes. The problem of the people's sin, injustice, and oppression leads to violence and bloodshed (Isaiah 5:7). But this vine story says nothing of sin. God has willed the growth of the vine (verse 8) and the destruction of it (verse 12). Both acts are equally mysterious. Hence, the anguished lament of a people who feel inexplicably rejected by God.

Psalm 80:14-19. The community cries out for renewed protection for the vine. They vow that when God "revive[s them]" they will "call on [God's] name" (verse 18). The fourfold refrain emphasizes the plaintive seriousness of the prayer (verses 3, 7, 14, 19).

Psalm 83. Ancient history is again called to mind to face a modern crisis.

Psalm 83:1-4. A conspiracy against Israel is afoot. Many neighboring nations are joined together to destroy Israel as a nation.

Psalm 83:4-8. This list of nations reads like a most wanted list for Israel. At no time in Israel's history did all of these nations conspire together against Israel. Indeed these nations did not even exist at the same time in history. But, in the psalmist's imagination, the rogue's gallery has joined together to plot the final defeat of the people.

Psalm 83:9-12. The psalmist knows God can defeat the enemies of Israel, because God has done it before. The psalmist refers to the Book of Judges and to an ancient hero and an ancient heroine whose great victories were won over enemy conspirators with the help of God. First, Deborah's victory over Sisera, the general of Jabin's army, is recalled (see Judges 4–5). Next, Gideon's victory over the Midianites is mentioned. As God has acted in these great victories, may God act again.

Psalm 83:13-18. This conspiracy theory leads to powerful curses on those who would dare to plot against Israel. Death is willed for all the participants in the plot (verse 17).

Psalm 90. This psalm wrestles powerfully with the question of human mortality and the brevity of life. But instead of finding the despair of Psalm 39, this psalmist finds strength and certainty in a life rooted in God's eternal being.

Psalm 90:1-2. God has always been God and has always been the refuge of the people.

Psalm 90:3-6. The shortness of human life is a common biblical theme (see Isaiah 40:6-8). In God's sight, human life is brief indeed, but this fact is no cause for sorrow.

Psalm 90:7-12. The psalmist says it is simply a fact that human life is only so long and no more. Human life is short because of sin. In the face of God's awesome eternal nature, humanity can only feel a conviction of sin and weakness (see Isaiah 6:5). But the psalmist's request to God is not abject surrender or weak resignation. Verse 12 is the key line that shows the psalmist's attitude.

> Let us know to number our days,
> in order that we might gain a heart of wisdom.
> *(my translation)*

A healthy recognition and acceptance of one's mortality leads to the wisdom we all hope to gain. Life is brief, but when rooted in God life can be full and glad.

Psalm 90:13-17. A simple request is made here. One finds no desire to break the heads of the wicked or to curse them into an early grave. The psalmist asks God to provide gladness and favor. The psalmist also asks God to establish the psalmist's humble, human work. The request is earnest (verse 13). This request is quite different from the often violent ones we have heard in other lament poems.

Psalm 126. This poem was almost certainly written during the exile of Judah (the Southern Kingdom). The psalmist directs God to restore Zion.

Psalm 126:1. I would translate this verse, "When Yahweh brings back the returnees to Zion, we are like dreamers." When the great day arrives and Judah can leave its exile and return home again, the dreams of the people will be rekindled. New hope will arise.

Psalm 126:2. Laughter and songs of joy will characterize the returning Judahites. Other nations will freely admit that "the Lord has done great things for them."

Psalm 126:3. We can only agree with this statement. God has done great things for us, but greater things will appear.

Psalm 126:4-6. Here the psalm echoes the great words of Isaiah 55:12-13. Weeping will turn to shouts of joy. Seeds will burst forth into sheaves. Here the psalmist is asking God to restore our fortunes (verse 4) when God restores the fortunes of Zion (verse 1).

Psalm 137. I want to make certain that you clearly understand the interpretation of this psalm. This psalm is a paean to hate. Verses 7-9 make that clear. But the reasons for hate are very important and not so self-evident.

Psalm 137:1-3. The people of Judah are definitely in Babylonian Exile (587–538 BC). They can only weep over the loss of Zion. They hang up the instruments they used to sing praises to God. But their captors demand music from the exiles so they can make fun of it.

Psalm 137:4. Now comes the key verse. "How do we sing Yahweh's song on a foreign soil?" (my translation). The answer of this psalmist is, "We cannot." Our answer must be, "We can." God's song is invariably found on foreign soil where it is rejected, scorned, avoided, denied, forgotten. Precisely at that point is when we must sing.

Psalm 137:5-6. But these singers cannot sing. They long for Jerusalem and for the safety, security, and certainty of God's temple. If only we could get back to God's temple, they say. Then we could sing! But who couldn't sing in the place where all are expected to sing? Rather than keep their faith alive with a new song, the psalmist turns to hatred and rejection.

Psalm 137:7-9. Blind wrath replaces faith. The nostalgia for Jerusalem replaces the vitality of God in a new land. Under such circumstances, death is the only way for those who only long for "the good old days." Those days are often more old than good.

DIMENSION THREE: WHAT DOES THE BIBLE MEAN TO ME?

Psalms 74, 84, 137—Responses to Crisis

The Exile in Babylon and the destruction of Jerusalem were shattering experiences for Judah. In many ways, it was the chief crisis of Israelite history. Let me suggest other responses to this crisis that the Bible records to add to those I mentioned from the communal laments of this lesson.

- The god of Babylon has beaten Yahweh, the God of Israel. By all outward appearances, Marduk was a stronger god than Yahweh, whose land and temple were now gone. Isaiah 46:5 satirizes the false gods of Babylon who in no way can compare to Yahweh, even though it seems otherwise. Have we allowed appearances to dampen our allegiance to God and God's will for us? Do we act as if Marduk, the god of this world, is in fact victorious over our God?

- Yahweh has forsaken Israel. This was a common response to the crisis of exile, fully consistent with many of the laments we have read. Lamentations 5:19-22 puts this response most painfully. Isaiah rejects this view. God could no more forget Israel than a nursing mother could forget her nursing child (Isaiah 49:14-15).

- The Exile was God's judgment on a sinful Israel. The earlier prophets had warned of God's impending judgment. The Exile seemed to confirm their warnings. Isaiah also records this view (Isaiah 42:24; 43:24; 46:8). But Isaiah 40 proclaims that God has forgiven all those sins and now offers comfort rather than judgment.

- Perhaps God is not quite who we thought. This seems to be the question of Job. If righteousness is not always rewarded and wickedness not always punished, then what is the universe really like, and what sort of God is running it? God may be more mysterious and surprising than we have imagined.

- Who cares anyway? If the Exile can happen, perhaps life is empty and meaningless. So says Ecclesiastes, whose first words about the brevity of all life provide a picture of life's emptiness.

The ancient Israelites took the crisis of the Exile with real seriousness. They did not deny the crisis. When a crisis is denied, we can offer no response nor can we move beyond the morass of the present. Do you face your crises squarely and honestly? Or do you deny the crises in your life? Do you find in these answers to crisis answers that you give or have given to crises? What other answers are possible? Which one do you find most fruitful?

Close the session by reading together Psalm 74:12-17.

For the LORD watches over the way of the righteous, / but the way of the wicked leads to destruction (1:6).

12

WISDOM PSALMS

DIMENSION ONE:
WHAT DOES THE BIBLE SAY?

Answer these questions by reading Psalm 1

1. How can a person be blessed? (1:1-2)

    A person can be blessed who does not walk in step with the wicked but delights in the law of the Lord.

2. How does the psalm describe this happy one? (1:3)

    This happy one is like a fruitful tree.

3. What are the wicked like? (1:4)

    The wicked are like chaff that the wind blows away.

Answer these questions by reading Psalm 37

4. Why should we not worry about the wicked? (37:2)

    They will soon wither like green plants.

5. Why should we have patience? (37:10)

    In a little while the wicked will be no more.

6. Where does the salvation of the righteous come from? (37:39)

    The salvation of the righteous comes from the Lord.

Answer these questions by reading Psalm 49

7. Who is addressed in the psalm? (49:1-2)

All who live in this world are addressed.

8. Why should we not fear those who trust only in wealth? (49:7-9)

They can never redeem the life of another or ransom life at any cost; thus they will "see decay."

9. From where will God ransom the psalmist? (49:15)

God will ransom the psalmist from the grave (Sheol).

Answer these questions by reading Psalm 73

10. Why did the psalmist have feelings of envy? (73:3)

The psalmist was envious of the prosperity of arrogant and wicked people.

11. How did the psalmist regain true faith in God? (73:17)

The final destiny of the wicked was revealed in the sanctuary.

12. How does the psalmist describe himself? (73:22)

The psalmist claims to have been a brute beast, senseless and ignorant, before knowing God.

Answer these questions by reading Psalm 78

13. How does the psalmist propose to speak? (78:2)

The psalmist will speak in parables.

14. How does the psalmist describe the forebears of Israel? (78:8)

They were stubborn, rebellious, and not loyal to God.

15. What is God's last act recounted in the psalm? (78:70-71)

God chose David to be king ("shepherd of his people Jacob").

Answer these questions by reading Psalm 91

16. Who is the person who is safe from peril? (91:1)

    The one dwelling in the shelter of the Most High is safe.

17. How will God guard your ways? (91:11)

    God will command his angels to guard you.

18. How will the psalmist know that God has given salvation? (91:16)

    The psalmist will have a long life.

Answer these questions by reading Psalm 127

19. Who must always build the house? (127:1)

    The Lord must always build the house.

20. Is rising early and going to bed late helpful? (127:2)

    No, it is vain; for God grants sleep to those he loves.

21. What makes a person happy? (127:4)

    Having many children makes a person happy.

Answer these questions by reading Psalm 133

22. How should God's people live? (133:1)

    They should live in unity.

23. What is the unity of God's people like? (133:2)

    The unity of God's people is like precious, dripping oil.

DIMENSION TWO:
WHAT DOES THE BIBLE MEAN?

The psalms to be covered in this lesson are Psalms 1, 37, 49, 73, 78, 91, 127, and 133. Psalms 112, 119 and 128 are the same type of psalms, but will not be considered in this lesson.

The Old Testament wisdom tradition is usually referred to as one of "rationalism." The words *intellectual enlightenment* are often used. One of the chief concerns of these authors was to educate people to live their everyday lives usefully. Thus, brief maxims of practical advice are a staple of this literature. However, we should not allow the words *rational* and *enlightenment* to suggest that there was nothing of God in the literature. The Wisdom Literature was not a sort of secular humanism of the past; God infuses the literature from beginning to end. But the questions that are raised and the religious doubts expressed are real and profound. Not just practical information is involved but also literature of the most highly theoretical and speculative kind. In the wisdom psalms, this diversity is well represented. Psalms 37, 49, and 73 are examples of the theoretical. Psalms 127 and 133 are eminently practical. Old Testament Wisdom Literature permeates every age of Israel's written record from early to late because the questions raised are questions for every time and for all time.

Psalm 1. The basic question of the psalm will be: "Who are the righteous in the sight of God and who are the wicked?" Other questions follow about the relationship between the two and what happens to them. Thus, it is fitting that the psalm opens the Book of Psalms. This psalm was probably never used in worship. It was composed as a summary of the book it heads.

Psalm 1:1. The words *blessed* and *happy* are usually interchangeable in the Bible. However, the basic meaning is *happy*. The precise interchangeability is also found in the beatitudes of Jesus (see Matthew 5). Religiously speaking, the truly happy one is the blessed one. To be truly happy, one must neither walk, stand, nor sit with the wicked. A moment's thought indicates that all postures are included by the three verbs. No contact with the wicked must occur. The word *mockers* is a bit unusual, following the much more common *wicked* and *sinners*. It appears to mean those who boast of their deeds in arrogance. The wicked not only do sinful things, but they also brag about it.

Psalm 1:2-3. The stark contrast of the meditating righteous and the boastful wicked is noteworthy. Actually, the word translated *meditate* means "to reflect aloud or to think about and mutter." You have perhaps seen pictures of Orthodox Jews studying the Torah. They mutter quite loudly as they probe the text for its meaning. A righteous Jew delights in and studies the Torah day and night. For Christians, the faithful study of God's word is also a key to righteous behavior. The one who studies becomes a deep-rooted tree that bears fruit. A colleague of mine once said that "sermonettes make Christianettes." That is, sweet talks about religion do not lead to real faith. Only profound study can lead to profound faith.

Psalm 1:4-6. The wicked are the very opposite of the deep-rooted tree of the righteous. The wicked are the chaff that needs to be blown out of the good grain before it is useful. These wicked cannot remain in the congregation of the righteous. They are alien and take no delight in the Torah.

Psalm 37. The psalmist is witnessing to a belief that has very little basis in reality. But the psalmist's belief is heartfelt and attempts to answer that most troublesome of biblical questions: Why do the wicked prosper? The answer is that they do not prosper for long.

Psalm 37:1-7. If this poetry seems choppy and disjointed, you are seeing it correctly. This psalm is an alphabetic acrostic. (See also Psalms 9–10; 34; 112.) The unity of thought is not crucial. The artificial device of the acrostic is designed to aid the memory for teaching. "Do not fret because of those who are evil," cries the author, "they will soon wither."

Psalm 37:8-22. The wicked are described in traditionally despicable ways. They especially commit that foul deed of "bring[ing] down the poor and needy" (verse 14). A crime we have seen over and over again, it is the very lowest kind. But no matter how foul they are, the wicked perish. They vanish like smoke (verse 20). One need only wait patiently for their inevitable demise (verse 10).

Psalm 37:25. As simplistic and naive as this claim certainly is, it provides for us the clue as to just what sort of psalm this is. A didactic psalm, it is designed to teach something. The prosperity of the wicked is a scandal in a universe ruled by a just God. Our orthodox teacher merely asserts that the righteous do gain their reward, while the wicked get their just deserts. The psalmist tells us that by believing in divine retribution we can maintain faith and moral equilibrium. In this way, we can avoid the great turmoil evidenced by Psalm 73.

Psalm 49. On the surface, this psalm appears to be a very rational, intellectual attempt to solve a difficult question of theology. The wicked are rich, they boast of their riches, and the psalmist is terrified of their power. However, this psalm, like Psalm 73 as we shall see, is tied to the worship of Israel, even if in an unusual way.

Psalm 49:1-4. All people, low and high, rich and poor, are called to listen to the solution to this vexing question. The translation "low and high" is literally "children of 'Adam, children of 'ish." Whether that actually means "low and high" is difficult to determine. ('Adam equals humanity, and often so does 'ish.) Whatever the precise meaning of the phrase, it certainly includes everybody. The psalmist speaks in a verbose and pretentious way. This tone is fully characteristic of the wisdom authors. The psalmist then names the main problem by using two very familiar wisdom words, riddle (hidah) and proverb (mashal) or parable. A riddle indicates a matching of wits. A concealed meaning needs to be discovered.

The most famous example of an Old Testament riddle comes from the story of Samson. Samson asks his almost in-laws a riddle. (See Judges 14:14.) The answer is wheedled out of Samson's bride by the distraught Philistines who cannot imagine the answer of "honey" and "lion" (Judges 14:18). Later the prophets develop this riddle form into clever and serious poems attacking the evil of Israel (see Isaiah 5:1-7 for an example).

The parable/proverb is a much broader term. We often think of the parables of Jesus, which are in effect longer adaptations of the form that is quite diverse in the Old Testament. It can be nearly synonymous with a riddle (see Proverbs 1:6; Ezekiel 17:2). It can be longer discourses of the wise (Numbers 23–24).

Note, also, that the psalmist in verse 4 is going to solve the riddle to the music of his harp or lyre. Because the lyre (kinnor) is a traditional instrument in the worship of Israel, we can assume that our psalmist found the solution during worship, either in the sanctuary or in an ecstatic or mystical state.

Psalm 49:5-6. The power that the wealthy wicked have held over the psalmist has caused the poet to be terrified. The psalmist is terrified not only of the power itself, but also of the implications for justice that the prosperity of the wicked indicates. Psalms like this are deadly serious. If the wicked really do prosper, then in what sort of universe do we live? There must be final justice if the world is to have meaning and if God is to be worshiped as supreme judge. (See Genesis 18 for a narrative that addresses this question of final justice.)

Psalm 49:7-12. The prosperity of the wicked is not forever. The parable is solved when the psalmist states two harsh facts about life. In verse 7, the first fact is stated. Let me translate it literally.

> No one can ransom a brother;
>> One cannot pay God his price.

That is, you cannot purchase anyone else's life, nor can you buy your own. This leads to the second fact: All persons die and go to the pit. Even the wise die. The author of Ecclesiastes concludes from this fact that life is meaningless (Ecclesiastes 3:19-20). The psalmist finds comfort in the fact. Different authors interpret things in different ways!

Psalm 49:13-15. The difference between the wicked and wise is that the death of the wicked is cruel and untimely. This seems to be the implication of verse 14. The wise psalmist will be saved from mortal danger (verse 15). This verse is not a statement of immortality. The psalmist has earlier affirmed the universal demise of all (verse 10). The psalmist can only claim that the death of one is more unpleasant than the other.

Psalm 49:16-20. The poet concludes by exhorting others to remember and proclaim that "you can't take it with you."

Psalm 73. This psalm asks, If God is just then why are there inequities in the government of the world?

Psalm 73:1. This statement of orthodoxy is both a confession of faith and a claim to be debated for the wisdom teacher.

Psalm 73:2-3. This psalmist admits doubt in the face of the world's wickedness.

> I was jealous of the boasting
>> when I saw the shalom of the wicked.
> (my translation)

How can the wicked have *shalom* when God's will is for the *shalom* of the righteous?

Psalm 73:4-12. The *shalom* of the wicked seems complete. These cynical, wicked people grow fat on their brazen crimes. This is in such sharp contrast to the promises of Psalm 1:4-6 that the psalmist is in serious danger of rejecting belief in God. After all, do not the wicked have a skeptical attitude toward God, an attitude that leads directly to their gross immorality (verse 11)? And they are comfortable!

Psalm 73:13-16. If such wickedness is not punished, then why bother to be good (verse 13)? Only suffering comes from being good (verse 14). Who wants to suffer? When the wise poet tried to employ all the intellectual tools he possessed, it was only wearisome and finally useless (verse 16).

Psalm 73:17. But here comes the turning point for the psalmist. The psalmist enters the sanctuary of God and there learns the true fate of the wicked. The fate of the wicked is described as appropriately terrible and swift. In Hebrew this is literally translated as sanctuaries. The wise one includes in the revelation not just the worshiping place but also those institutions connected with the sanctuary. This would surely have included schools. Thus, the revelation to the psalmist comes not only in worship, but also in study. In other words, the psalmist returns to the orthodox places of school and temple to have his faith restored.

Psalm 73:18-20. The wicked die quickly and horribly, as the usual wisdom school doctrine affirms.

Psalm 73:21-28. After this return to the fold of faith, the poet laments past ignorance (verse 22). Then the psalmist affirms that only God is the source of justice and strength forever.

Psalm 78. The question of theodicy (the just God and a world of evil) is presented here in the form of a hymn. The author wants to prove to us that God has acted in history. History has taken this particular way, and that way was God's way, which is always just.

Psalm 78:1-8. This psalm is clearly didactic, as are most of the wisdom psalms. The same two Hebrew words, translated "parables/proverb" and "riddle," used in Psalm 49 are used to describe the content of this psalm. (See verse 2. "Hidden things, things from of old" literally means "riddle.") We must remember and transmit to future generations the history lesson we are about to receive (verse 5). They should "put their trust in God" (verse 7) and avoid the terrible stubbornness and rebellion of their ancestors (verse 8). We might phrase it this way: Those who do not study history are condemned to repeat it.

Psalm 78:9-33. The argument of this long history lesson is in reality quite simple. Verses 9-11 tell that the tribe of Ephraim forgot God's covenant and the miracles God showed them. The poet says that they "turned back on the day of battle" (verse 9). We do not know what incident is referred to here. The reference to Ephraim is another way of referring to Israel. Ephraim was the northern part of the country when it was divided into two sections after the death of Solomon (922 BC). The people of Ephraim saw God's power in the Exodus from Egypt (verse 11) and received the law at Sinai (verse 10), but they rejected it all. Thus, God rejected them. Verses 12-33 give a long, dismal record of Ephraim's rejection of God's actions on its behalf.

Psalm 78:54-60. Even the gift of the Promised Land was not enough to prevent Ephraim's rebellion against God. So, God rejected Israel (that is, the Northern Kingdom, verse 59), and God destroyed Shiloh, a sacred sanctuary of the North. Jeremiah 7 refers to this destruction and uses it as proof to Judah, the Southern Kingdom, that God is not bound to preserve any sanctuary, no matter how sacred. Here it is proof of God's disapproval of Ephraim.

Psalm 78:67-72. Now God's purpose in this long history is made clear. God rejected "the tents of Joseph" (another name for the Northern Kingdom) and chose the tribe of Judah and its Jerusalem sanctuary (Mount Zion). In this way, the destruction of the Northern Kingdom of Israel by the Assyrians in 721 BC is explained as God's activity. And, David, the greatest king of Israel, and all his descendants are now God's special people forever. So, the divine history lesson ends with the moral that history is of God. Obedience is required to maintain a relationship to that God.

Psalm 91:1-2. Those who pray that God is "my refuge and my fortress" will rest in the shadow of the Almighty. In the Jewish *Kaddish* prayer for the dead, they are said to "reside in the shadow of the Most High," an apparent mixing of the two lines of Psalm 91:1.

Psalm 91:3-10. No matter how terrible life can be, no matter the depth of life's horror, God will provide refuge (a verb from the same noun of verse 2) under God's wings (verse 4). God's feathers (pinions) is an image used only twice in the Old Testament. The other use of it is in Deuteronomy 32:11. There God, as here, plays the role of the protective bird who finds and shelters the people.

Psalm 91:11-12. That these lines should appear in the story of Jesus' temptation is appropriate. (See Matthew 4:6 and Luke 4:10-11.) The devil quotes those words to tempt Jesus to employ the power of God for his own use. This gives a delightful ironic twist to that New Testament story. The devil speaks of protection but twists God's promise of protection into a temptation to use power.

Psalm 91:13-16. The priest now offers the divine promise to the faithful in the first person. The psalm is obviously used in the service of worship at this point.

Psalm 127:1-2. "Unless the LORD builds the house / the builders labor in vain." This proverb is expanded by quoting two more proverbs that make a similar point. If God does not protect a city, no watchman can ever fully protect it. If you work hard, it will do you no good unless you can experience God's restful sleep.

Psalm 127:3-5. "Children are a heritage from the LORD, / offspring a reward from him." The second proverb in this psalm is then expanded to show why children are so important as God's gift. The loose unity of these two expanded proverbs is God's presence and active concern in all of life's affairs.

Psalm 133:1. Here again we have an extended proverb. "How good and pleasant it is / when God's people live together in unity!" This idea is important and seems to refer to the specific family unit. "God's people" ("Brothers" in the NRSV and in NIV 1984) thus means "close family relative." The unity of the family is very important for the survival of society.

Psalm 133:2. A long beard dripping with precious oil is the first image the poet uses to indicate the beauty of the unity of God's people. The manly beard and the precious oil joined together give a potent metaphor of the unity of God's people. This unity is strong and beyond price. The mention of Aaron adds sanctity to the image.

Psalm 133:3. The dew on the beautiful Mount Hermon, matched by the dew on the sacred Mount Zion, demonstrates again the beauty and sanctity of the unity of God's people. As the oil drips down, as the dew comes down, so God's blessing falls down from Zion and gives life to the faithful, especially those who dwell in unity.

DIMENSION THREE:
WHAT DOES THE BIBLE MEAN TO ME?

Why Do the Wicked Prosper?

This question assumes the fact that there is a moral order governing the universe. If such is a fact, then why do the righteous suffer and the wicked prosper? We have looked briefly in the participant book at the answers of Psalms 37, 49, and 73. Let us now examine the other ways the Old Testament dealt with this profound problem.

Job apparently resigns to God the reality that the answer to the question is deniably a divine, but mysterious one. As we saw in Lesson 11, the author of Psalm 44 attacks God quite directly for neglecting the people. Psalm 44 recognizes the problem is God's and demands that God act to solve the difficulty. We have seen that the most common response is that God does finally vindicate the righteous against the wicked. (See Psalms 34:6 and 50:15, for example.) Late in the Old Testament, authors began to consider that wrongs may not be righted in this life. They thought wrongs might be corrected on some day of judgment when all injustice would be straightened out (see Isaiah 3:14-15 and Daniel 12:1).

Perhaps the prosperity of the wicked and the righteous suffering as a result of it were designed to cause the righteous to return to God with renewed devotion. (See Psalms 20:6 and 39:7 for an example of this idea.) This idea then led to the idea of the righteous suffering on behalf of others in some sort of vicarious way (see Isaiah 53).

One can see by this brief sketch that the Old Testament had no easy answers to provide to this question. I have none either. However, it is a question well worth careful consideration. How one approaches this question will have a large effect on the way one approaches the question of the nature of God. How does this biblical survey help you in addressing the question? Ask class members how they go about explaining disasters like tornadoes or floods. How do they respond in relation to God's will? When persons of ill repute gain fortunes and die apparently happy, how do they explain it? Or do they explain it?

The LORD is my shepherd, I lack nothing (23:1).

13
PSALMS OF CONFIDENCE

DIMENSION ONE:
WHAT DOES THE BIBLE SAY?

Answer these questions by reading Psalm 11

1. What is the advice given to the psalmist? (11:1)

Some tell the psalmist to "flee like a bird to your mountain."

2. Does the psalmist accept the advice? (11:4)

No, because God is in "his heavenly throne."

3. What will God do to the wicked? (11:6)

God will rain fiery coals and burning sulfur on the wicked and send a scorching wind.

Answer these questions by reading Psalm 16

4. What does the psalmist refuse to do? (16:4)

The psalmist will not run after other gods or participate in pagan rites.

5. Why is the psalmist's heart glad? (16:10)

The psalmist is glad because God does not abandon him to the grave.

Answer these questions by reading Psalm 23

6. How is God described in the psalm? (23:1)

God is described as a shepherd.

7. Why does God lead in the right paths? (23:3)

God guides in the right paths for the sake of God's name.

8. Who witnesses God's table preparation for the psalmist? (23:5)

The enemies witness God's preparation.

Answer these questions by reading Psalm 131

9. What has the psalmist not done? (131:1)

The psalmist has not been concerned with great and wonderful things.

10. What is the psalmist's mood? (131:2)

The psalmist is calm and quiet.

Answer these questions by reading Psalm 50

11. Who does God want to gather? (50:5)

God gathers "this consecrated people."

12. Does God desire Israel's animal sacrifices? (50:9-13)

God has "no need" for animal sacrifices.

13. What is the sacrifice that honors God? (50:23)

Thanksgiving is the sacrifice that honors God.

Answer these questions by reading Psalm 68

14. What does the psalmist hope happens to the wicked? (68:2)

The psalmist wants the wicked to perish as smoke vanishes in the wind and as wax melts in a fire.

15. How is God best known in the psalm? (68:5)

God is father of the fatherless and defender of widows.

16. How can one escape death? (68:20)

>   *The Sovereign Lord saves and provides escape from death.*

Answer these questions by reading Psalm 81

17. How should God be praised? (81:1-3)

>   *God should be praised by music and feasting.*

18. What does God specifically reject? (81:9)

>   *God rejects any foreign god in Israel.*

19. What would happen if Israel would listen to God? (81:14)

>   *God would subdue their enemies for them.*

Answer these questions by reading Psalm 82

20. Where is God in the psalm? (82:1)

>   *In this psalm, God presides in the great assembly.*

21. What is wrong with the other gods? (82:1-2)

>   *The other gods defend the unjust and show partiality to the wicked.*

22. Does the psalm deny the existence of other gods? (82:6-7)

>   *No, but the other gods are reduced by Yahweh ("the Most High ") to mere men who will die like all other men.*

DIMENSION TWO: WHAT DOES THE BIBLE MEAN?

The psalms we will study in this lesson are four psalms of confidence, Psalms 11, 16, 23, 131, and four miscellaneous psalms, 50, 68, 81, and 82. Psalm 62 is also a psalm of confidence, but will not be considered in this lesson.

As we approach this final lesson on the Book of Psalms, we want to consider how we can use these psalms to enliven our own worship and prayer lives. More will be said about this in Dimension Three, but we need to be attentive to the way we examine the psalms. Their literary unity and formal structure have been very important to us and can lead to more appropriate ways to use them in worship. Also, of course, their unique contents, from hymn to lament, can help us decide how to use them most appropriately. For example, the psalms of confidence can prove valuable in prayer and worship when studied correctly.

Psalm 11. This psalm has a very contemporary tone. The psalmist is faced with dangerous enemies. Some well-meaning friends advise the poet to run from the enemies. The rest of the psalm is a rejection of that advice, based on confidence in God.

Psalm 11:1-3. The psalm begins with the psalmist expressing confidence in God. The poet affirms his faith and then explains why running from enemies is not what one should do. The advice is to "flee like a bird to your mountain" (verse 1). In other words, go far away to a high place, removed from the enemies who have apparently taken over the earth. The key line is verse 3:

> When the foundations are ruined,
> > what can the righteous do? (my translation)

The Hebrew word translated here as foundations is a rare one, used only three times in the Old Testament. In 2 Samuel 10:4 and Isaiah 20:4, it refers to the human buttocks and the shame of the buttocks being uncovered in public. Here it must mean that which is basic to all things of society. If the bases are destroyed, society is doomed and the righteous are helpless. Is not our society saying much the same? We are in serious trouble, so flee to yourself, to your success, to your money. After all, what can the righteous do? The psalmist responds with a powerful refusal to flee.

Psalm 11:4-7. The psalmist reminds those who would flee that God remains in the temple and on the throne of heaven. God watches the activities of all (verse 4). God hates violence (*hamas*). The word *hamas* represents the evil actions of injustice and oppression. God's answer to violence is to rain coals and sulfur (fire and brimstone) on the wicked. Burning sulfur also was used to describe God's destruction of Sodom and Gomorrah in Genesis 19:24. Power from on high dealt with the evil of the cities, remembered as places of violent oppression. Because God is righteous and loves justice (verse 7), the righteous must not flee, but must stand with the righteous God.

Psalm 16. The Hebrew text here is really quite poor. But if verse 4 can be understood at all, it stands at the center of the psalmist's problems.

Psalm 16:1. As in Psalm 11, the psalmist begins with a faith claim: "In you [God] I take refuge." And also as in Psalm 11, the psalmist's antagonists are described and rejected.

Psalm 16:4. This verse is important. Let me translate it as literally as I can.

> After they hasten, they increase their images;
> > but I will not pour out their bloody libations;
> > I will not put their names on my lips.

It seems certain that the psalmist is rejecting the gods of the other peoples, whoever they are. These gods apparently require some sacrifices of blood (required in the worship of Yahweh, too) and the public proclamation of their names (also required in Yahweh worship). But it is not the kind of worship that is offensive. The object of the worship is what is objectionable.

Psalm 16:5-8. In contrast to these unnamed heathen gods, verse 5 begins with the name of God. God is the "portion and cup" of the psalmist. In other words, God is the psalmist's food and drink. Further, God made "my lot secure." Casting lots is often a magic way to discover the will of God. (See Jonah 1:7 and 1 Samuel 10:20.) Its most common use is for the selection of the sacrificial animal in Israel's worship. (See Leviticus 16:8-10.) In this context, the *lot* means "destiny." The psalmist affirms that God controls destiny, not any of the heathen gods. Verse 6 refers to the lines that mark off landed property. The psalmist equates valuable real estate to God's destiny, as when Daniel is promised his "allotted inheritance" (Daniel 12:13). To be sure, this psalmist has never confronted the tragedy of Job or the agony of the author of Psalm 39.

Psalm 16:9-11. The psalmist is now secure in God. He has no fear of death nor any particular concern about it. God's way is the path of life (verse 11) and does not point to Sheol ("the grave"). The psalmist does not deny death here. The psalmist merely denies that death has any power. We can learn from this psalmist. Being preoccupied with dying can lead us to a deathlike life. God is most interested in living, not dying.

Psalm 23. What words could possibly be added about Psalm 23? This psalm is such a familiar and powerful part of Christian piety that it fairly resists analysis. But as often in biblical study, to know something in greater detail is to love and appreciate it all the more.

Psalm 23:1-3. In the first brief verse, the content of the poem is given. "The LORD is my shepherd." The implication is that I am a sheep and that the leader is known by me and recognized by me as my leader. "I lack nothing." With God as shepherd, I have all I need of real and lasting value. God leads in "green pastures" by "quiet waters." These bucolic images paint pictures of calm, especially for those of us who find ourselves living far from both. God "refreshes my soul." That is, God provides the reason and excitement for living. All of this is done for God's "name's sake" (verse 3). God leads, guides, and protects because God is that sort of God. From this God you can expect this kind of activity.

Psalm 23:4. God is present even in the glen of gloom. We need not be paralyzed by fear no matter how terrifying the problem may appear. Even if the familiar translation, "valley of the shadow of death" is not quite accurate, the point of God's reassuring presence is the same.

Psalm 23:5. The images of ease and comfort of verses 1-3 and the image of danger of verse 4 are now joined together in an image of a banquet spread in the midst of the enemies. Danger is everywhere, but the banquet is rich and luxurious. Calm is everywhere.

Psalm 23:6. The psalmist vows at the end of this psalm of confidence to return to God's sanctuary as long as the psalmist is alive. God's wonderful goodness and love (our familiar Hebrew word *hesed*) will pursue us always. In response to that loving pursuit, we go back to God's house again and again to praise.

Psalm 131:1. The appropriate first approach to God is not fist-shaking, says this author, but lowered eyes and a humble heart. Personally, I am a better fist-shaker than I am an eye-lowerer. I often find myself pursuing things too great and awesome for me. I do not think this means we need to deny our intellects or the pursuit of knowledge. It does say we need to pursue things that are proper and useful for the purposes of God.

Psalm 131:2. "Surely, I have calmed and silenced myself" (my translation). My, do I need to do that! My life is filled with excited words but little calm and silence. I can learn from the "weaned child." Although the child is no longer suckling its mother, the child is stilled by her presence and can fall calmly and contentedly asleep.

Psalm 131:3. In Israel, the psalmist wants these same calming experiences. The Hebrew reads literally, "Wait, O Israel, for Yahweh, both now and forever." Wait in humbleness and wait in calm quiet. I think this psalmist speaks to me as much as to Israel. Don't you hear the psalmist speaking, too?

Miscellaneous Psalms

Psalms 50, 68, 81, 82. These last four psalms bear little resemblance to one another and not much resemblance to any particular psalm form. They all seem to have some connections to specific worshiping experiences, but we cannot be certain. They truly are miscellaneous poems in the Psalter.

Psalm 50. This psalm was profoundly influenced by the prophetic lawsuit of God against Israel and the concern with the appropriate sacrifice to God.

Psalm 50:1-6. This language is of course borrowed from the hymns of Israel. (See, for example, Psalm 18:7-15.) The God who comes in judgment is described with images of the greatest power. Fire and tempest or wind (verse 3) are common images. (See 1 Kings 18–19; Exodus 32.) God then summons the consecrated people "who made a covenant with me by sacrifice" (verse 5). (In other places the NIV has translated consecrated people as "your own people/faithful servants" [see Psalms 79:2; 85:8].) This seems to suggest that those who in good conscience connect themselves to God through animal sacrifice need to hear again what God really desires of them.

Psalm 50:7-21. The indictment begins. This use of hymnic and legal language is very reminiscent of Amos 4:1-5, 13. In Amos, God calls out the indictment against Israel and then is described in powerful hymnic language to make the indictment even more potent. (For other examples of prophetic indictments, see Isaiah 1:2-3 and 42:18-25.) God accuses Israel of making sacrifices into substitutes for true religion. God does not reject animal sacrifices. (Amos seems to assume God does in Amos 5:21-24.) But the reasons for those sacrifices have become confused. Some claim to pay God with sacrifice. But God retorts that creatures are God's (verse 11). Some claim to feed God with the sacrifice, but God denies any actual hunger (verses 12-13).

What God wants is thanksgiving. This word means a song of thanksgiving that accompanies an admittance of sin and leads to confession. (See Joshua 7:19 and Ezra 10:11 for examples of where this movement from thanksgiving to confession occurs.) This thanksgiving also involves the vow and the payment of the vow (verse 14). What God wants, most clearly, is a heartfelt change of spirit rather than external acts of worship.

Some scholars have suggested that the first line of verse 16 has been added to modify the poet's judgment against the whole nation to a judgment against the wicked only. This claim is hard to sustain, given the nearly constant distinction in the psalms between the righteous and the wicked. In verses 16-21, the wicked are barred from the worship service because of evil in society.

That society's evil makes true worship impossible is another traditional prophetic theme. We need to hear and reflect upon this harsh idea.

Psalm 50:22-23. The poem ends with a warning (verse 22) and with a promise (verse 23). The warning is that God can tear like an animal at those who forget. But to those who truly bring the sacrifice of thanksgiving, God will demonstrate salvation.

Psalm 68. Being really helpful when trying to explain this enigmatic poem is difficult. Its connection to worship is obvious, but confusing. It appears not to have any form. We note references to history in this psalm, but many of them are lost to us. We can only point to a few places for comment.

Psalm 68:1-3. The call "May God arise" that opens the psalm is a request for a theophany, an appearance of God. The wicked need to be defeated, and only God can do so.

Psalm 68:4-6. The congregation now picks up the call to praise God. God is described in exciting, though traditional ways.

Psalm 68:7-10. A comparison of verses 7-8 to Judges 5:4-5 is interesting. Note that in the Judges passage God is located as coming from Seir and Edom, places clearly to the south of Israel. In the psalm, the geographical references have been changed to general statements concerning God's activities before the people and the "wilderness." The pouring rains in the Judges passage lead to the flooding and destruction of the armies of Sisera. In the psalm, the rain leads to the restoration of God's inheritance (verse 9). Here we find an unusual transformation of original Old Testament material.

Psalm 68:11-23. Note the references to "Mount Bashan" in this section. Bashan is first envious of the mountain of God, presumably Jerusalem (verse 16). Then, God vows to "bring them from Bashan" (verse 22), as if some of God's enemies who needed especially cruel judgment were there.

Psalm 68:24-27. The mention of just these four tribes in the festal procession is peculiar. Two tribes are of the south, Benjamin and Judah. And two tribes are from Galilee, the north, Zebulun and Naphtali. Is the poet trying to be inclusive of the whole country?

Psalm 68:28-35. Now God's power and wealth are proclaimed. (Verse 30 is virtually impossible to read in Hebrew text.) Finally, God rides in the heaven (verse 33), but is also connected to the holy sanctuary (verse 35). What this psalm originally meant appears lost to us.

Psalm 81. This psalm was composed for the great feast day of the Jews, sometimes called the Feast of Tabernacles or Booths. The celebration was held in the autumn at the close of the agricultural year. (See Deuteronomy 16:13-15 for a general command to celebrate this feast.)

Psalm 81:1-5. The community is summoned to the feast. The song is to be sung, the worshiping instruments played (verse 2). The ram's horn or trumpet (*shofar*) is to be blown to begin the festival and call the worshipers together. Celebrating the feast is obeying God's "decree and ordinance" (verse 4).

Psalm 81:6-10. The prophetic voice brings the word of God directly into the feast. God has acted in the past "out of a thundercloud" (Sinai), at the waters of Meribah (Exodus 17:7; Numbers 20:13), and at the Exodus from Egypt (verse 10). But these persons did not listen. They worshiped strange gods (see Exodus 32).

Psalm 81:11-13. They did not listen to God. They would have none of God. The implication is that these contemporary witnesses must listen to God. If they do not, God will hand them over to their "stubborn hearts" (verse 12). The Hebrew word used here for *stubborn* is only found a few times in the Old Testament and always in connection with "the heart." The heart was considered the seat of intellect and the will for the Hebrews. The past Israelites have been afflicted with this stubbornness. The present ones need to avoid it.

Psalm 81:14-16. If they do avoid it, God will subdue their enemies. I would translate verse 15, "Those who hate Yahweh will flatter Yahweh, / their (life) will be forever." In other words, I think it means that even the enemies will turn to God eventually, because the Israelites listened to the voice of God. The beginning of verse 16 reads in Hebrew, "he would feed him." This apparently refers to the reconciliation of the enemies who now feed Israel with the finest of wheat. God provides all with the honey of satisfaction. Thus the harvest festival becomes a sacred drama where God converts the enemies to friends because of the obedience of the Israelites.

Psalm 82. This psalm boldly employs the theme of the victory of one god over other gods. The defeated gods are then demoted to mortality.

Psalm 82:1. God summons the divine court and proceeds to mete out justice to the lesser gods who have failed in their responsibilities.

Psalm 82:2-7. These gods who were to bring about justice have done nothing of the kind. They have instead brought darkness to the earth and have shaken the earth to its very foundations (verse 5). Because they have failed to bring justice, they will die like any human being. They shall "fall like every other ruler" (verse 7).

Psalm 82:8. Then God is left to judge the earth. The psalmist calls on God to arise, requesting God's appearance in judgment.

This psalm is a dramatic account of the victory of the God of Israel over all the other gods of the nations. What we see here is a long struggle to understand the God of Israel as unique and alone in the universe.

DIMENSION THREE: WHAT DOES THE BIBLE MEAN TO ME?

The Use of the Psalms in Worship

Here are several ideas you might want to discuss with the group about using the psalms in the worship services of your church. Let me begin with the obvious.

- The approach to the psalms that looks carefully at the literary form of each psalm should help in the proper selection of a psalm for the proper time in the service. The types of psalms we have examined follow the acts of worship in our services: Adoration (hymns), Penitence and Petition (laments), Assurance (psalms of confidence), Thanksgiving and Dedication to Service (many possible psalm types).

- The most expendable part of most worship services is the responsive reading of the Psalter. Why? Because it can become monotonous and mechanical.

But if we follow the shape of the psalm itself, other patterns for recitation are possible. For example, Psalm 42–43 has a choral refrain as we noted. (See Psalm 42:5, 11; 43:5.) Why not break the responsive reading into that natural shape? Why not have the choir sing a response to a composed tune? Ask class members to name some other possibilities.

- Do not edit out theological parts of the psalm you think are objectionable. Objectionable sections are usually crucial parts of the psalm's content and movement. The psalms do come from a different time than our own. However, we do them no service to try to make them conform to our way of thinking rather than to try to understand them.

Have class members look at Psalm 24 (we studied it in Lesson 3). Ask them to compose a responsive reading based on this psalm, using what they have learned about literary form and shape. Then close the session by using what they have written.

Let me add my prayer for you:

O God of power and love, help us to feel your presence as we search for you in our lives. Help us to know that we have already been found by you and loved by you. Grant us *shalom* in our time. Amen.

CPSIA information can be obtained
at www.ICGtesting.com
Printed in the USA
LVHW01s0350250817
546275LV00009B/19/P

9 781501 848391